THE GAME PLAN

D1568780

THE GAME PLAN
Governance With Foresight

John B. Olsen
Douglas C. Eadie

SUSAN WALTER, GENERAL EDITOR

Studies In Governance
Volume One

THE COUNCIL OF STATE PLANNING AGENCIES

HALL OF THE STATES
400 NORTH CAPITOL STREET
WASHINGTON DC 20001

On the cover: *Way to the Citadel* by Paul Klee. Courtesy of The Phillips Collection, Washington, D.C.

© 1982 by The Council of State Planning Agencies

Library of Congress Cataloging in Publication Data

Olsen, John B.
    The game plan.

    (Studies in governance)
    Bibliography: p.
    Includes index.
    1. State governments. 2. Planning. I. Eadie, Douglas C. II. Council of State Planning Agencies. III. Title. IV. Series.
JK2443.04   353.9'17'2   82-7378
                                                             AACR2
    ISBN 0-934842-20-5

Book and Cover Design by Chuck Myers
Typography by Wordscape

Manufactured in the United States of America

The Council of State Planning Agencies is a membership organization comprised of the planning and policy staff of the nation's governors. Through its Washington office, the Council provides assistance to individual states on a wide spectrum of policy matters. The Council also performs policy and technical research on both state and national issues. The Council was formed in 1966; it became affiliated with the National Governors' Association in 1975.

Funding support for this volume was received from the National Science Foundation. The views and findings it contains are the authors' and do not necessarily represent those of the National Science Foundation or the members or staff of the Council of State Planning Agencies. Reproduction of any part of this volume is permitted for any purpose of the United States Government.

The Council of State Planning Agencies
Hall of States
400 North Capitol Street
Washington, D.C. 20001
(202) 624-5386

About the Authors

JOHN B. OLSEN is senior vice president at Mellon Bank, where he is responsible for developing and operating the strategic planning system which serves the chief executive officer of that international commercial bank.

Previously, Mr. Olsen was the director of the Office of Budget and Management (OBM) of the State of Ohio. He was appointed by Governor John J. Gilligan to head and develop this cabinet department, newly created to succeed the Department of Finance. In that position, he was responsible for structuring OBM to perform three principal executive functions: budget policy development and control; management improvement; and planning and evaluation. Prior to joining state government, Mr. Olsen was the assistant director of the Cleveland Foundation, where he served as the chief administrative and financial officer of this community trust with assets over $200 million and dedicated to serving community needs. Earlier in his professional career, he had been a senior project manager with the international management consulting firm of Booz-Allen and Hamilton.

Mr. Olsen received the B.A. degree from the University of Illinois and the M.S. degree from the School of Management at Case Western Reserve University. He has regularly been a lecturer on corporate planning at the Graduate School of Business of the University of Michigan, is currently the president of the Pittsburgh Chapter of the

North American Society for Corporate Planning, is listed in *Who's Who in Finance and Industry,* serves on the Corporate Planning Executive Committee of the American Bankers Association, and has been elected a member of the National Academy of Public Administration.

DOUGLAS C. EADIE is currently engaged in research and consulting in the fields of strategic planning and executive management while on sabbatical leave from the position as executive assistant to the chancellor of Cuyahoga Community College. In his capacity at the College, he has acted as chief of staff of the Chancellor's Office and has been responsible for a comprehensive management improvement program, including the implementation of a long-range planning system, financial and budget management, and computer support.

Previously, Mr. Eadie served as director of the Management and Budget Services Divison of the Ohio Department of Public Welfare, which had an annual budget of nearly $1 billion. He established, staffed, and managed the Management and Budget Services Division, directed the preparation of the Department's biennial budget, and initiated a wide-ranging financial management system development project. Prior to joining state government, Mr. Eadie was director of the Bureau of Management and Budget of the City of Portland, Oregon. Earlier in his career, he was deputy executive director of the Greater Erie Community Action Committee of Erie, Pennsylvania, which involved him in the role of chief administrative officer of a $4 million annual budget community development agency, and before that had been a teacher with the Peace Corps in Ethiopia.

Mr. Eadie received the B.A. degree with distinction from the University of Illinois, where he was inducted into Phi Beta Kappa and Phi Alpha Theta, and the M.S. degree from the School of Management at Case Western Reserve University. He has lectured on the subject of business policy analysis at the Graduate School of Business at Portland State University and on general management at Cuyahoga Community College. He has written several speeches, papers, and articles on strategic management.

Foreword

TO HEAR ALARMS of impending calamity is becoming
commonplace. To gain a comprehensive, balanced understanding of the means available for addressing the contemporary issues confronting governance is indeed rare and
refreshing. It is precisely because this book is so timely,
focused, and pertinent to shaping a positive response to the
evident dilemmas that confront our society that I commend it
to the broadest possible readership of my colleagues in the
private sector.

I doubt that there is a person in the business community
who hasn't been approached to provide some form of assistance to government. Of course, businesses do pay taxes and
in that way provide direct assistance. But increasingly, there
are requests for loaned executives, grants to sundry public
projects, and support for a myriad of local community
activities. Without extensive research, it is possible to observe
that these requests are numerous and growing; in view of
emerging Federal policies, they are likely to burgeon well
beyond the capacity of the private sector.

Perhaps this is a unique opportunity. While the requests are
being made for new funding, I suggest that the business
community may be instrumental in helping accomplish some
positive results from an admittedly bleak situation. Rather
than risking being overwhelmed by requests beyond our
means, or dissipating resources through indiscriminate token
contributions, we could give first priority to strengthening and
improving state governments. There are many reasons to do
so, not the least of which are the following:

• The problems which confront governments are shared by

business; common efforts may be expected to be reinforcing and serve to overcome the problems introduced by a diminishing public revenue base.

- Business could gain a greater understanding of the public sector's sense of values, decision-making processes, and the complexities of contemporary public administration.
- The prospect of working at the level of state government has much which is attractive: the number of governments is manageable, the economies of scale are more easily realized, and the results should be both appreciable and replicable to some degree at the county/city level.

To do anything less than undertake such leadership now is to invite serious risk. We have all reaped the benefits of an enterprise economy and stable democratic government; a quick scan of the daily newspaper should provide convincing evidence that these salutary conditions are not to be taken for granted. As a nation, we can expect to experience serious economic problems over the next decade which may challenge the foundations of our political, social, and economic systems. Human and financial investment by the business community in state government is both prudent and compelling; in the short term to avoid the cost of inefficiencies, and in the long term to assure the survival of this enterprise economy that has bestowed the highest standard of living in history.

Fletcher L. Byrom
Chairman of the Board
Koppers Company, Inc.

THE ECONOMIC ENVIRONMENT of the 1980s has forced
state government to seek new and innovative ways to provide
essential governmental services to its citizens, while simul-
taneously coping with diminished financial resources.

To successfully accomplish this objective we must have a
clearer perception of future demands and resources; we must
establish new directions for state government that will enable
us to lead rather than to only react to change; and we must
develop and implement mechanisms that will reduce inefficiencies, encourage innovation, permit effective decision
making in the face of turbulence, and insure that our actions
are in the long-term best interests of all citizens.

This is no small task for state government. The only realistic
way that it can be accomplished is through the rigorous application of strong planning and management techniques, such
as those embodied in the concept of strategic planning.

It is my belief that the primary purpose of planning must be
to improve the quality of day-to-day decision making. An
effective strategic planning process will permit the formulation
of a consistent set of policy decisions and actions which, over
time, will result in the achievement of longer-range objectives.
In short, strategic planning helps to produce basic decisions
which become the criteria that guide and shape all future
actions and activities of state government.

In Pennsylvania, we have taken the initial steps to apply the
principles of strategic planning to state government. My
concern with Pennsylvania's economy and its prospects in the
decade of the 1980s prompted my request to the Pennsylvania
State Planning Board to initiate a strategic planning program
called *Choices for Pennsylvanians.* My particular interest was
in identifying and implementing economic measures that
could improve Pennsylvania's overall economic climate by
providing more jobs and job opportunities in the Commonwealth, and also conserving and helping to revitalize our
communities which have been hit hard by business and
industrial disinvestment.

In the course of carrying out this strategic planning
program, the State Planning Board established long-range
economic goals and objectives for Pennsylvania; carefully
assessed Pennsylvania's economic future, identified specific
problems, resources and opportunities and formulated a set of
alternative scenarios of the future to assist the state in under-

standing the implications of various day-to-day policies and actions. The Board solicited advice and opinions from many institutions and experts, and a citizen participation program was carried out to assure that it had the views of Pennsylvanians from every part of the Commonwealth.

To me, the value of strategic planning lies in the prospect of being able to cut through the morass of issues and problems that impede the achievement of our objectives in state government. While no amount of planning can relieve the burden of decision making, strategic planning can help to focus on our most critical concerns, more clearly identify our alternatives and their consequences, and help insure that the actions we ultimately select are geared to producing a future environment of our choosing, one that will meet the social and economic needs of our citizens.

This book, prepared under the auspices of the Council of State Planning Agencies, provides guidance to states that wish to embark on a strategic planning program. It is clearly the most comprehensive work to date on strategic planning in the public sector, and I believe that public officials will find it of significant value in helping to meet the management challenges of state government in the 1980s.

Dick Thornburgh
Governor of Pennsylvania

Contents

The Game Plan

Introduction

One cannot disregard the challenges faced by state government today. Whether by design or coincidence,the devolution of functional responsibilities from the Federal government coupled with the yet undiminished expectations of citizens toward governmental services constitute a new threat for the management capability of state governments. As the ramifications of such new Federal policies (moving from categorical programs to block grants; minimizing Federal mandates; withdrawing from the support of selected social programs) are recognized, and the implications of relatively static economic growth are weighed, the fiscal, managerial, and political capacities of state government are due to be sorely tested—perhaps as never before. Tighter budgets and the need for greater discretion in responding to volatile conditions that require prompt action dramatize the requirement for priority setting and more effective organizations.

The conditions for applying strategic planning in government have long been inviting; now the reasons to do so are compelling. In addition to the imperative for greater rationality in public sector decision making and program performance, emerging economic factors and Federal policies help create fundamental and difficult public policy choices that demand a coherent and defensible basis for decisions. Those management disciplines that may have once appeared to be a luxury are fast becoming an essential prerequisite for survival at the state and local levels of government.

With this in mind, the traditional, and altogether practical, purpose of this introduction is to place the subject of this book in perspective: to lay out the roadmap for the reader who will journey with these authors to the destination of understanding better how strategic planning may be usefully applied in state government today. While this is intended to be a balanced exposition of the techniques and demonstrated value of strategic planning, it is not without a point of view. We intend to support our conclusion that, to ensure a responsible and effective administration of state government, a governor needs to develop an explicit and durable statement of strategy, review it periodically and discuss it broadly, use it as a reference source for gubernatorial decisions, and share with the cabinet and legislative leadership the risks associated with its adoption.

Yet a journey such as this is not without some perils: there is as much need to spark informed interest as there is to guard against quackery. We even gave fleeting consideration to avoiding the term "planning," for it has got a bad reputation in some quarters. The alternative terms such as "anticipatory analysis," however, lacked redeeming qualities. So we are resigned to offer this essay without benefit of euphemism, ever trusting that the reader will be tempted to explore the topic less in the hope of finding a fashionable panacea than in the search for a means to render government more effective as consistent with the values of a democratic tradition. Succinctly stated, strategic planning is a disciplined effort to produce fundamental decisions shaping the nature and direction of governmental activities within constitutional bounds.

This current age is characterized by rapid and constant change. That governmental organization isn't well structured to respond to such turbulence gives rise to serious problems. It is observed that the present public sector decision-making apparatus is best suited to dividing up an ever-increasing resource pie, but does not contemplate stasis or decline. How then are crucial, timely decisions to be made, a consensus developed that enables policy change, and confidence built in the capabilities of the system and the staff charged with implementing policies over a period that may span a number of years? In this situation, criticism of government abounds and undermines further the capacity and resolve to deal with contentious matters. Perhaps no circumstance so clearly demands leadership, and the governor may be uniquely equipped to provide it. Indeed, defining the "problem" is always far more important than devising the solution, for a problem's definition dictates the range of possible remedies that might be imagined. In a simple schematic, figure 1 depicts the basic planning process which will be described and analyzed in subsequent chapters.

As the majority of states rely on an apparently inadequate resource base in responding to citizens' demands for increased effectiveness and expansion of services, the quality of management in state government is an ever more critical issue. It is our belief that no aspect of management looms larger than the planning function in enhancing public and private management. Therefore, the opportunity to examine for the Council of State Planning Agencies the potential for applying strategic planning and management in state government was greeted with enthusiasm. One of the foremost challenges in preparing this study was to present the principles, techniques, and practices of strategic planning and management in a fair, complete, and accurate fashion while also communicating effectively with our primary audience. Although we have no doubts that strategic planning and management, if properly applied, can be a valuable tool to use in shaping state directions and policies, and generally in managing state government, we have attempted to present a balanced view, avoiding the "oversell" so common in the introduction of new technologies and techniques. Admittedly, and we think fortunately, our extensive public and private sector management experiences have armed us with a healthy skepticism in approaching the topic.

We are keenly aware of the tendency of many mana-

FIGURE 1

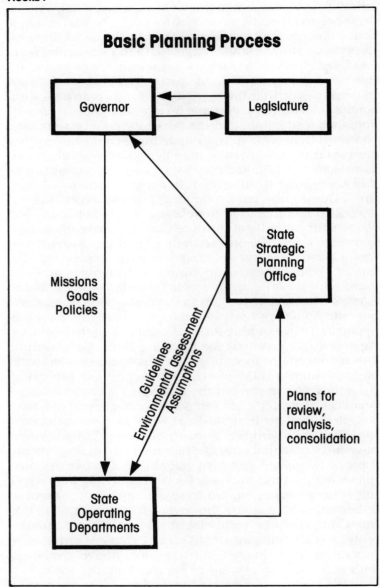

Basic Planning Process

gers to hail and embrace new management tools—such as Program Planning and Budgeting System, Management by Objectives, and Zero Base Budgeting—in an alarmingly uncritical fashion. This tendency to view such potentially valuable tools as panaceas, while underestimating the costs of realizing their benefits, invites certain disillusionment and likely failure. Thus, due care is required. Strategic planning and management possess great potential for enhancing the operation of state government, especially as the issues become more complex and interrelated, thus demanding more sophisticated management approaches. However, that potential can be fully achieved only if there is a clear understanding of both the limitations and the full cost of implementation.

In preparing this book, we have been guided by the need to provide always busy and often harrassed state executives with useful guidance in tapping the potential benefits of strategic planning. We have focused on bridging the gap between the theory of strategic planning, such as it is, and the process of actually putting it into practice. In this respect, our book should serve as a guide or handbook for state managers in applying the logic and principles of strategic planning in their unique situations. It is intended to be useful to the governor and his staff, the operating department managers, legislative leaders, and students of government.

In constructing such a practical guide, we have attempted to avoid the pitfall of oversimplification. Strategic planning is a means for focused, analytical, and orderly decision making: it requires the explication of alternatives; forces a future orientation; encourages broad-scale information gathering and evaluation; provides for communication and participation; emphasizes the importance of implementation; and can be tailored to accommodate different organizations characterized by divergent purposes and values. In brief, it has been shown to confer apparent and substantial advantages. Nonetheless, we seek to emphasize at the beginning, as we shall reiterate at the conclusion, that motivation is of paramount importance in promoting the effectiveness of large scale organizations; the process of strategic planning presents an opportunity to help employees at all levels of government recognize the broader goals and challenges that lend meaning and give value to their own jobs, jobs that may otherwise be seen as trivial and routine. As the Japanese have recently and convincingly demonstrated, attention to the motivation of employees can deliver impressive productivity gains and improved organizational performance.

To proceed with this exposition, we have developed the book in three chapters aimed at affording the would-be practitioner with information in a readily usable manner.

☐ Chapter 1 constitutes the foundation. It serves to identify and describe the principal components of strategic planning, present major reservations and caveats in order to build a balanced perspective on the subject, and illustrate the significance of these factors. Rather than attempt to construct a single, comprehensive model, the aim here is to provide the reader with a central theme and major variations—a theoretical framework that is detailed enough to assist in designing practical applications in the state government context.

☐ Chapter 2 explores the transition from the largely private sector-oriented theory and experience in strategic planning to the unique needs, requirements, and circumstances of state government today.

☐ Chapter 3 addresses the issues surrounding implementation of strategic planning and provides state officials and managers with some candid advice. Major implementation options are identified and assessed, and approaches to organizing the planning function are discussed. Following is a set of appendixes that contain useful examples that can aid directly in implementation activities.

We hasten to acknowledge the insightful advice and criticism provided by colleagues during our preparation of this study; hence we share the credit for this work (and whatever merit it possesses), while we alone are accountable for its shortcomings. This manuscript benefited from the review and comments of James A. Norton, Edward F. R. Hearle, Harold A. Hovey, Larry C. Ledebur, and Carl W. Stenberg. Our experience in state government, served in the administration of Governor John Joyce Gilligan of Ohio, has imparted a special appreciation for the practitioner who must implement the policies and programs—however grandiose or mundane—by which all institutions operate. The staff of the Council of State Planning Agencies deserves mention for its thoughtful and persistent efforts to broaden the understanding of planning and to advance its application; several Council board members have readily provided information and interviews; and Susan Walter has been a most perceptive and engaging editor of this manuscript. The encouragement and support of Janet Bennet Eadie greatly facilitated the contribution of Douglas C. Eadie to this joint effort.

And finally, we must single out for very special acknowledgment our teacher and dear friend, Professor Nathan D. Grundstein. His eloquently, and frequently, articulated abhorrence of the conventional wisdom—however artfully disguised—more than once stayed our hand when we were tempted to commit a platitude to paper. His vision of management as a noble art and science, transcending its several functional specialties, and his intense commitment to democratic values have inspired us to set our sights higher than we otherwise might. The extent to which we may have succeeded only the reader can judge.

Survey of the Theory and Practice of Strategic Planning: A Review of Current and Professional Experience

The Historical Context

IIII▶ Formal long-range planning is a relatively recent development in the history of management. Prior to 1960, very few corporations had adopted long-range, or corporate, planning systems; since then, however, long-range planning has become a widely accepted and utilized management tool in the private sector. The major "waves of adoption" came from 1962 to 1965 in the United States and from 1964 to 1969 in Europe.[1]

It is sensible to think of strategic planning as a more sophisticated version of long-range planning, responding to new planning needs and requirements. In little over a decade, strategic planning has come into its own, at least in terms of having become a recognizable field, subfield, or discipline within professional management education, if not in terms of actual formal practice in private or public management. Even though there is no conclusive evidence that formal strategic planning systems have been widely implemented, no self-respecting executive is likely to admit to being without conscious strategies—be they grand master strategies or more narrowly focused ones involving products, functions such as marketing, research and development, or geographical areas. It is fashionable these days for executives to converse in the "lingo" of strategic planning, distinguishing readily between activities truly strategic in significance from those more mundane or "tactical."

Despite having barely emerged from its infancy, strategic planning is experiencing such rapid growth and change that it is extremely difficult to keep abreast of the field. Even to read a good part of the burgeoning academic and more popular literature is a real challenge. Several new books appear every year, and hardly an issue of *Business Week* or the *Harvard Business Review* appears without an examination of some firm's strategic goals or a closer look at one of the strategic planning functions. Even the hallowed business policy course, long the capstone for graduate students in many of the nation's business schools, is slowly but surely evolving into the study of strategy formulation and implementation.

A "snapshot" of the field of strategic planning at any given time quickly becomes a source of nostalgia, appealing principally to those of historical bent. Every day sees the theoretical foundation grow richer and more variegated as new dimensions are added and older ones seen in different perspective. Advances in technology and technique succeed each other with bewildering speed. He who attempts to present strategic planning in a neat nutshell is surely brave, and most likely foolhardy. There are serious students of planning today who even suggest that we may already have entered the postformal strategic planning system era, forced by rapidly increasing environmental turbulence, characteristic of what Drucker has called the "Age of Discontinuity," to adopt more flexible responses.

Whether or not a fundamentally new kind of planning is emerging, it is clear that the rapidly increasing rate of environmental change since the 1950s, and especially over the past decade, has led to many of the important changes in the technology and process of strategic planning—to greater flexibility and more frequent updating of plans, to such techniques as "alternative future environmental scenarios," and to such analytical aids as the portfolio approach to resource allocation.[2]

It is to the history of the development of the American industrial enterprise since 1900 that one must look in attempting to understand the emergence of long-range and then strategic planning. Specifically, one must focus on the variety of dynamic relationships between the internal context of a firm and its wider external environment—physical, economic, technological, social, and political. A widely respected planning scholar, Professor H. Igor Ansoff, sees the first major developmental phase as the "Mass-Production Era," when the focus of management was on increasing the efficiency of production. During this first stage, from roughly 1900 to the 1930s, the external environment of the firm was relatively stable and favorable to the expansion and refinement of the production function. Government intervention was rare, most frequently involving action to nurture and protect industrial development and less often to preserve competition through enforcement of antitrust legislation. Despite growing union strife through the period, the prevailing social mores offered no serious challenge to the expansion of industrial production. The planning function in this context was understandably oriented toward the control of both production and costs, relying on rudimentary management reporting, based largely on accounting data.[3]

The succeeding "Mass-Marketing Era," roughly extending from the mid-1930s through the mid-1950s, brought with it a shift from "an internally focused, introverted perspective to an open, extroverted one," much more attuned to consumer tastes and desires. It was during this stage of development that long-range planning based on extrapolative forecasting began to take root, although as noted above, the adoption of formal long-range planning systems proceeded very slowly, with widespread adoption not occurring until the 1960s.[4]

Since the mid-1950s, according to Ansoff, we have been passing through a period of transition to what he terms the "Post-Industrial Era." This transitional period has been characterized by rapid developments in planning theory and technology as a means of coping with increasing environmental turbulence, whose "accelerating and cumulating events" have begun to alter the "boundaries, the structure and the dynamics of the business environment."

> To summarize briefly, during the past twenty years, a major escalation of environmental turbulence has taken place. For the firm it has meant a change from a familiar world of marketing and production to an unfamiliar world of strange technologies, strange competitors, new consumer attitudes, new dimensions of social control and, above all, a questioning of the firm's role in society.[5]

Adversity, real and imagined, has certainly acted as a powerful fertilizer in the field of planning during this period. It has yielded bountiful advances in planning theory and technology, and has promoted their widespread application. Strategic planning, building on an increasingly solid long-range planning foundation, has developed rapidly. If the future seems murkier—less predictable and more threatening—one can at least take consolation knowing that the tools available to us are fast becoming more sophisticated.

Some Basic Definitions

There is broad agreement in the literature as to the meaning of such terms as "strategic," "strategy," "strategic planning," and "strategic management." There are, however, numerous variations on the general themes and considerable disagreement about the specifics of content, structure, and process. For the purposes of this book, broad working definitions are used and major variations are introduced only when essential to a balanced understanding of a concept. Complexity for its own sake is avoided.

Whether a matter is strategic, or more functional—operational or tactical—is obviously relative, having to do with the degree of focus on ends and the period of time affected. Russell Ackoff puts the distinction simply: "The longer the effect of a plan and the more difficult it is to reverse, the more strategic it is."[6]

Strategies are obviously the principal intended outcomes of strategic planning, which is by definition the process of formulating strategies. Generally speaking, strategies are positioned on the intersection of an organization with its external environment, present and future, in such a way that the organization's resources are used most effectively in adapting to that environment. The overall objective is to make the most of current or anticipated environmental conditions while capitalizing on opportunities and narrowing constraints.

According to business historian Alfred Chandler, a strategy is the "determination of the basic long-term goals and objectives of an enterprise, and the adoption of courses of action and the allocation of resources necessary for carrying out these goals."[7] George A. Steiner, perhaps the dean of planning scholars, has stated that strategic planning should deal with "anything that is highly important to the success of the company," including, among other elements, coping with environmental forces, capitalizing on advantages, repulsing threats, and identifying new opportunities.[8] Another respected teacher and scholar of planning, Richard F. Vancil, has written that strategies are the "primary source of cohesiveness" in an organization.[9]

King and Cleland have proposed a very useful definition of the work of strategic planning, focusing on the elements of organizational purpose, orientation toward the future, and environmental forces:

> Strategic planning is that element of a manager's job and of the organization's function that deals with the contrivance of change, rather than the simple reaction to it. Strategic planning involves those choices related to overall organizational purposes, oriented toward the future, and importantly involving uncontrollable environmental forces. Strategic choices are those that emphasize future missions and future generations of "product" outputs and resource inputs. In contrast, the organization's day-to-day operating environment emphasizes current objectives and the existing generation of outputs and resources.[10]

Strategies come in a wide variety of kinds, shapes, and sizes. At the highest level, there are overall "master" or "enterprise" strategies within which narrower strategies are developed. Aside from scope, strategies can focus on such areas as growth objectives, product, market, financing, and pricing. One should not overlook personal strategies that, according to the authors of a respected text on management policy and strategy, "constitute a fundamental, and generally unwritten, framework within which business strategy is developed." As the authors point out, the higher the organizational status of the manager, the more important his or her strategies are to the affairs of the firm. To consider the process of strategy formulation without this personal dimension would lead to an incomplete understanding of the dynamics.[11]

Some Caveats

Formal long-range, or corporate, planning and strategic planning tend to be treated as one and the same, but there are instances when making a distinction between the two processes will be useful in understanding more clearly what strategic planning is all about. It appears all too common, at least in the public sector, for formal long-range planning to become in practice highly ritualistic, contributing little to the formulation of strategy for the organization. Even though they frequently go through all or most of the standard motions, planners in such systems focus on documenting, and perhaps refining, current activity. Although they may take a somewhat perfunctory glance at the external environment, the real starting point for these planners is usually internal—the existing statements of programmatic goals and objectives. Strategic options are not defined; hard choices among alternative directions are not made; trade-offs are not required. Quite the opposite, lengthy lists of aspirations and intentions are compiled into massive documents, conveying the impression that everything is possible.

Such formal planning processes are in clear contrast to strategic planning, the peculiar genius of which is its conscious, searching attention to environmental factors and its objective of arriving at an optimum, feasible match between internal capabilities and external environmental conditions. The cost of an elaborate planning system that fails to meet the strategic needs of an organization is likely to be very high, if not precisely calculable. Of the scarce time available, day-to-day operational demands are likely to command the lion's share, leaving longer-range thinking and planning a distinct second. If this time is consumed by a formal, ritualistic process that fails to meet the organization's needs, there will be little or no time left to do the planning that *is* required.

Another negative feature of an elaborate planning process that involves going through the motions without achieving strategic purposes is that the process gives the illusion of achievement. Such self-delusion can be inordinately risky in times of environmental turbulence. Certain major criticisms of formal planning systems will be explored later in this chapter.

It is not clear from the literature whether strategic planning and strategic management are the same or distinct processes. The consensus seems to be that strategic management constitutes the overall framework, within which strategic planning takes place, making the major contribution by generating the strategies to be managed. Two relatively recent works illustrate the definitional problem. Schendel and Hofer describe strategic management as a "process that deals with the entrepreneurial work of the organization, with organizational renewal and growth, and more particularly, with developing and utilizing the strategy which is to guide the organization's operations."[12] Steiner and Miner, observing that strategy is "the central and unique core" of strategic management, go on to point out that the formal long-range planning process in many firms has become the strategic planning process, which is "inextricably interwoven with the entire strategic management process. In effect, strategic planning is a new way to manage."[13] It is probably safe to assume that, when strategic management is discussed, it includes strategic planning, even if the two are not identical processes. However, one cannot so safely

FIGURE 2

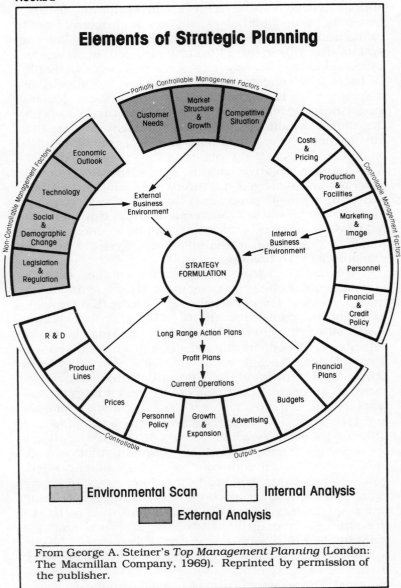

Elements of Strategic Planning

From George A. Steiner's *Top Management Planning* (London: The Macmillan Company, 1969). Reprinted by permission of the publisher.

assume that strategic planning incorporates everything meant by strategic management.

The Strategic Planning Process

It is generally agreed that the strategic planning process consists of the following basic components:

☐ The overall mission and goals statements, which are formulated by an organization's executive management and provide the framework within which strategies are developed—the "targets" toward which strategies are aimed.

☐ The environmental scan or analysis, consisting of the identification and assessment of current and anticipated external factors and conditions that must be taken into account when formulating the organization's strategies.

☐ The internal profile and resource audit, which catalogs and evaluates the strengths and weaknesses of the organization in terms of a variety of factors that must be taken into consideration in strategic planning.

☐ The formulation, evaluation, and selection of strategies.

☐ The implementation and control of the strategic plan.

As will be elaborated later in this chapter, there is considerable latitude in determining the degree of formality of the overall planning process, as well as of each of its constituent parts, and in determining the depth in which each step will be addressed. Decisions about the extent of formality and depth of performance depend on a variety of factors including the size of the organization, the diversity of its operations and complexity of its business, and the nature of its external environment.

1. Mission and Goals

The formulation of an overall mission and set of organizational goals is a critical element of the strategic planning process in that it provides a framework within which strategic planning takes place. In this introductory

FIGURE 3

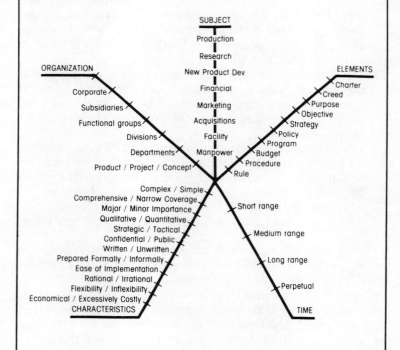

Five Key Dimensions
of Business Planning

SUBJECT
Production
Research
New Product Dev
Financial
Marketing
Acquisitions
Facility
Manpower

ORGANIZATION
Corporate
Subsidiaries
Functional groups
Divisions
Departments
Product / Project / Concept

ELEMENTS
Charter
Creed
Purpose
Objective
Strategy
Policy
Program
Budget
Procedure
Rule

Complex / Simple
Comprehensive / Narrow Coverage
Major / Minor Importance
Qualitative / Quantitative
Strategic / Tactical
Confidential / Public
Written / Unwritten
Prepared Formally / Informally
Ease of Implementation
Rational / Irrational
Flexibility / Inflexibility
Economical / Excessively Costly
CHARACTERISTICS

Short range
Medium range
Long range
Perpetual
TIME

From George A. Steiner's *Top Management Planning* (London: The Macmillan Company, 1969). Reprinted by permission of the publisher.

section, it would seem redundant to attempt to define what a mission or goal is or to describe the formulation process. Considerable attention has been accorded to the subject in the literature of long-range planning. It is important, however, to keep two points in mind relative to this stage in the process: first, that the statement of mission and goals that initiates the strategic planning process is not only the product of the organization's executive management, but is more importantly the unique expression of the chief executive officer's aims and expectations; second, that the mission and goals statements may change over the course of the strategic planning effort in response to the introduction of new information.

2. Assessment of the Environment

It is not unreasonable to consider that "getting a handle on" the current and future external environment of an organization is the most challenging step in the strategic planning process. Certainly none is more critical; strategic planning is, after all, basically the job of regulating a variety of relations between the internal and external environments of an organization—of making decisions in light of future possibilities. Indeed, as has been observed earlier in this book, it is the priority given to environmental analysis that distinguishes strategic planning from what many organizations do under the guise of long-range planning. The environmental scan or analysis may also be the most difficult facet of strategic planning to review in an introductory discussion because of the wide range of techniques being used and the rapidly changing technology.

Despite the increasing technological sophistication available to us in understanding and analyzing the external environment, it is essential to keep in mind that the function of forecasting the future is less a matter of scientific precision than of human judgment and intuition. As Uyterhoeven and his colleagues observe, the many factors to be considered and the difficulty of making predictions about many of them make strategic forecasting "by necessity . . . a highly uncertain process. It is one where judgments by reasonable people may vary significantly."[14]

FIGURE 4 Basic Forecasting Techniques

	A. Qualitative methods	
Technique	1. Delphi method	2. Market research
Description	A panel of experts is interrogated by a sequence of questionnaires in which the responses to one questionnaire are used to produce the next questionnaire. Any set of information available to some experts and not others is thus passed on to the others, enabling all the experts to have access to all the information for forecasting. This technique eliminates the bandwagon effect of majority opinion.	The systematic, formal, and conscious procedure for evolving and testing hypotheses about real markets.
Accuracy Short term (0-3 months)		
Medium term (3 months-2 years)	Fair to very good	Excellent
	Fair to very good	Good
Long term (2 years & up)	Fair to very good	Fair to good
Identification of turning points	Fair to good	Fair to very good
Typical applications	Forecasts of long-range and new-product sales, forecasts of margins.	Forecasts of long-range and new-product sales, forecasts of margins.
Data required	A coordinator issues the sequence of questionnaires, editing and consolidating the responses.	As a minimum, two sets of reports over time. One needs a considerable collection of market data from questionnaires, surveys, and time series analyses of market variables.
Cost of forecasting With a computer Is calculation possible without a computer?	$2,000 + Yes	$5,000 + Yes
Time required to develop an application & make a forecast	2 months +	3 months +
References	North & Pyke, "'Probes' of the Technological Future," HBR May–June 1969, p. 68.	Bass, King & Pessemeier, **Applications of the Sciences in Marketing Management** (New York, John Wiley & Sons, Inc., 1968).

These estimates are based on our own experience, using this machine configuration: an IBM 360-40, G.E. Time-sharing and IBM 360-30's and 1130's.

3. Panel consensus	4. Visionary forecast	5. Historical analogy
This technique is based on the assumption that several experts can arrive at a better forecast than one person. There is no secrecy, and communication is encouraged. The forecasts are sometimes influenced by social factors, and may not reflect a true consensus.	A prophecy that uses personal insights, judgment, and, when possible, facts about different scenarios of the future. It is characterized by subjective guesswork and imagination; in general, the methods used are non-scientific.	This is a comparative analysis of the introduction and growth of similar new products, that bases the forecast on similarity patterns.
Poor to fair	Poor	Poor
Poor to fair	Poor	Good to fair
Poor	Poor	Good to fair
Poor to fair	Poor	Poor to fair
Forecasts of long-range and new-product sales, forecasts of margins.	Forecasts of long-range and new-product sales, forecasts of margins.	Forecasts of long-range and new-product sales, forecasts of margins.
Information from a panel of experts is presented openly in group meetings to arrive at a consensus forecast. Again, a minimum of two sets of reports over time.	A set of possible scenarios about the future prepared by a few experts in light of past events.	Several years' history of one or more products.
$1,000 +	$100 +	$1,000 +
Yes	Yes	Yes
2 weeks +	1 week +	1 month +
		Spencer, Clark & Hoguet, **Business & Economic Forecasting** (Homewood, Illinois, Richard D. Irwin, Inc., 1961).

256 K system and a Univac 1108 Time-Sharing System, together with such smaller equipment as

Basic Forecasting Techniques (cont.)

Technique	B. Time series analysis & projection	
	1. Moving average	2. Exponential smoothing
Description	Each point of a moving average of a time series is the arithmetic or weighted average of a number of consecutive points of the series, where the number of data points is chosen so that the effects of seasonals or irregularity or both are eliminated.	This technique is similar to the moving average, except that more recent data points are given more weight. Descriptively, the new forecast is equal to the old one plus some proportion of the past forecasting error. Adaptive forecasting is somewhat the same except that seasonals are also computed. There are many variations of exponential smoothing: some are more versatile than others, some are computationally more complex, some require more computer time.
Accuracy	Poor to good	Fair to very good
	Poor	Poor to good
	Very poor	Very poor
Turning point Identification	Poor	Poor
Applications	Inventory control for low-volume items.	Production and inventory control, forecasts of margins and other financial data.
Data required	A minimum of two years of sales history, if seasonals are present. Otherwise, less data. (Of course, the more history the better.) The moving average must be specified.	The same as for a moving average.
Cost	$.005	$.005
	Yes	Yes
Time required to develop forecast	1 day –	1 day –
References	Hadley, **Introduction to Business Statistics** (San Francisco, Holden-Day, Inc., 1968).	Brown, "Less Risk in Inventory Estimates," HBR July–August 1959, p. 104.

3. Box-Jenkins	4. X-11	5. Trend projections
Exponential smoothing is a special case of the Box-Jenkins technique. The time series is fitted with a mathematical model that is optimal in the sense that it assigns smaller errors to history than any other model. The type of model must be identified and the parameters then estimated. This is apparently the most accurate statistical routine presently available but also one of the most costly and time-consuming ones.	Developed by Julius Shiskin of the Census Bureau, this technique decomposes a time series into seasonals, trend cycles, and irregular elements. Primarily used for detailed time series analysis (including estimating seasonals); but we have extended its uses to forecasting and tracking and warning by incorporating other analytical methods. Used with special knowledge, it is perhaps the most effective technique for medium-range forecasting—three months to one year—allowing one to predict turning points and to time special events.	This technique fits a trend line to a mathematical equation and then projects it into the future by means of this equation. There are several variations: the slope-characteristic method, polynomials, logarithms, and so on.
Very good to excellent	Very good to excellent	Very good
Poor to good	Good	Good
Very poor	Very poor	Good
Fair	Very Good	Poor
Production and inventory control for large-volume items, forecasts of cash balances.	Tracking and warning, forecasts of company, division, or department sales.	New-product forecasts (particularly intermediate- and long-term).
The same as for a moving average. However, in this case more history is very advantageous in model identification.	A minimum of three years' history to start. Thereafter, the complete history.	Varies with the technique used. However, a good rule of thumb is to use a minimum of five years' annual data to start. Thereafter, the complete history.
$10.00	$10.00	Varies with application
Yes	No	Yes
1-2 days	1 day	1 day −
Box-Jenkins, **Time Series Analysis, Forecasting & Control** (San Francisco, Holden-Day, Inc., 1970).	McLaughlin & Boyle, "Short-term Forecasting," AMA Association Booklet, 1968.	Hadley, **Introduction to Business Statistics** (San Francisco, Holden-Day, Inc., 1968); Oliver & Boyd, "Techniques of Production Control," Imperial Chemical Industries, 1964.

Basic Forecasting Techniques (cont.)

Technique	C. Causal methods	
	1. Regression model	2. Econometric model
Description	This functionally relates sales to other economic, competitive, or internal variables and estimates an equation using the least-squares technique. Relationships are primarily analyzed statistically, although any relationship should be selected for testing on a rational ground.	An econometric model is a system of interdependent regression equations that describes some sector of economic sales or profit activity. The parameters of the regression equations are usually estimated simultaneously. As a rule, these models are relatively expensive to develop and can easily cost between $5,000 and $10,000, depending on detail. However, due to the system of equations inherent in such models, they will better express the causalities involved than an ordinary regression equation and hence will predict turning points more accurately.
Accuracy	Good to very good Good to very good	Good to very good Very good to excellent
Turning point identification	Poor Very good	Good Excellent
Applications	Forecasts of sales by product classes, forecasts of margins.	Forecasts of sales by product classes, forecasts of margins.
Data required	Several years' quarterly history to obtain good, meaningful relationships. Mathematically necessary to have two more observations than there are independent variables.	The same as for regression.
Cost	$100 Yes	$5,000 + Yes
Time required to develop forecast	Depends on ability to identify relationships.	2 months +
References	Clelland, de Cani, Brown, Bush & Murray, **Basic Statistics with Business Applications** (New York, John Wiley & Sons, Inc., 1966).	Evans, **Macro-economic Activity: Theory, Forecasting & Control** (New York, Harper & Row Publishers, Inc., 1969).

3. Intention-to-buy & anticipations surveys	4. Input-output model	5. Economic input-output model
These surveys of the general public (a) determine intentions to buy certain products or (b) derive an index that measures general feeling about the present and the future and estimates how this feeling will affect buying habits. These approaches to forecasting are more useful for tracking and warning than forecasting. The basic problem in using them is that a turning point may be signaled incorrectly (and hence never occur).	A method of analysis concerned with the interindustry or interdepartmental flow of goods or services in the economy or a company and its markets. It shows what flows of inputs must occur to obtain certain outputs. Considerable effort must be expended to use these models properly, and additional detail, not normally available, must be obtained if they are to be applied to specific businesses. Corporations using input-output models have expended as much as $100,000 and more annually to develop useful applications.	Econometric models and input-output models are sometimes combined for forecasting. The input-output model is used to provide long-term trends for the econometric model; it also stabilizes the econometric model.
Poor to good	Not applicable	Not applicable
Poor to good	Good to very good	Good to very good
Very poor	Good to very good	Good to excellent
Good	Fair	Good
Forecasts of sales by product class.	Forecasts of company sales and division sales for industrial sectors and subsectors.	Company sales for industrial sectors and subsectors.
Several years' data are usually required to relate such indexes to company sales.	Ten or fifteen years' history. Considerable amounts of information on product and service flows within a corporation (or economy) for each year for which an input-output analysis is desired.	The same as for a moving average and X-11.
$5,000	$50,000 +	$100,000
Yes	No	No
Several weeks	6 months +	6 months +
Publications of Survey Research Center, Institute for Social Research, University of Michigan; and of Bureau of the Census.	Leontief, **Input-Output Economics** (New York, Oxford University Press, 1966).	Evans & Preston, "Discussion Paper #138," Wharton School of Finance & Commerce, The University of Pennsylvania.

Basic Forecasting Techniques (cont.)

	C. Causal methods (cont.)		
Technique	6. Diffusion index	7. Leading indicator	8. Life-cycle analysis
Description	The percentage of a group of economic indicators that are going up or down, this percentage then becoming the index.	A time series of an economic activity whose movement in a given direction precedes the movement of some other time series in the same direction is a leading indicator.	This is an analysis and forecasting of new-product growth rates based on **S**-curves. The phases of product acceptance by the various groups such as innovators, early adapters, early majority, late majority, and laggards are central to the analysis.
Accuracy	Poor to good Poor to good Very poor	Poor to good Poor to good Very poor	Poor Poor to good Poor to good
Turning point Identification	Good	Good	Poor to good
Applications	Forecasts of sales by product class.	Forecasts of sales by product class.	Forecasts of new product sales.
Data required	The same as an intention-to-buy survey.	The same as an intention-to-buy survey + 5 to 10 years' history.	As a minimum, the annual sales of the product being considered or of a similar product. It is often necessary to do market surveys.
Cost	$1,000 Yes	$1,000 Yes	$1,500 Yes
Time required to develop forecast	1 month +	1 month +	1 month +
References	Evans, **Macro-economic Activity: Theory, Forecasting & Control** (New York, Harper & Row Publishers, Inc., 1969).	Evans, **Macro-economic Activity: Theory, Forecasting & Control** (New York, Harper & Row Publishers, Inc., 1969).	Bass, "A New Product Growth Model for Consumer Durables," **Management Science**, January 1969.

Ironically, it appears that as the forecasting tools at our command grow in number and power, our capability to predict lessens, given an environment that "has rarely been exceeded in complexity, turbulence, rapidity of change, and significance of change. . . ."[15] The point, so easily forgotten, is that technology cannot substitute in this complex process for the trained mind and alert eye. All planners would be wise to heed the warning of the Carnegie Foundation for the Advancement of Teaching in its report *More Than Survival:*

> Assumptions, judgments, uncertainties—these are the stuff of which projections are made. It takes a dash of bravado to make a projection; but it shows a touch of madness to believe too much in its invincibility. We offer our projection as one possible guide to the murky future, knowing that it is only one guide among several that are being offered—and quite various they are. . . . The best advice to consumers of any of these projections, ours included, is *caveat emptor.*[16]

The first step involved in developing the environmental scan and related forecast is to identify the factors which appear to be relevant, either currently or potentially at some time in the future, to the particular organization. The specific list must obviously vary with each organization, but the number of factors that most large firms must consider has significantly increased over the past three decades. At a minimum, the list would include economic developments, technological changes, social values, the political climate, governmental actions, as well as factors traditionally considered, such as customer needs and desires and the nature of the competition. Merely selecting the factors to be measured and forecasted is a very small, though important, part of this first step. In the first place, it is impossible to formulate a list of mutually exclusive factors; the interrelationships are

29

inevitably many and highly complex. In the second place, any one factor is most likely a convenient label for a collection of related factors that, taken together, describe the composite factor. These subfactors may require different measurement and forecasting techniques: some may be amenable to reasonably precise projection; others may involve creative guesswork. Finally, the subfactors will vary in terms of the weight of their contribution to the composite factor.

What does it mean, for example, to talk about the state of the economy five or ten years hence? Do we mean the national, regional, state, or local economy? Do we talk of the GNP, total employment, the rate of unemployment, capital creation, or business growth (which itself involves a variety of measures)? What are the connections among political and social attitudinal changes and governmental action? Do we mean legislative enactments or presidential leadership at the Federal level? What about local and state government or regional authorities?

Once an organization has identified a package of external environmental factors on which it will concentrate in the strategic planning process, it then takes two further steps in the environmental analysis process: forecasting how the factors are likely to change over a future period and assessing the likely impact of those changes on the organization. A recent study of environmental analysis and forecasting concluded that assessment of impact or effect lagged behind advances in forecasting. In spite of the "burgeoning popularity and growth" of environmental forecasting and its "enthusiastic reception" in business and government, the author suggested that its usefulness was "severely constrained in practice" because predicting the effects of trends and events was "much more difficult than seeing the primary changes themselves."[17]

Information System Development

King and Cleland point out that firms have frequently focused on short-term control needs in designing management information systems and have tended to neglect planning information requirements. This has resulted "in the creation of sophisticated systems for collecting, processing, and disseminating internally generated information for control purposes . . . , whereas relatively unsophisticated systems suffice for coping with critical planning-related information." In their discussion of how an organization might approach the design of a strategic information system, they make a very useful distinction between strategic data, referring to "*unevaluated* available symbols," and information, which consists of data evaluated as useful in strategic planning. They caution organizations not to over-rely on internally generated planning information, even though it is easier to obtain, because of the growing importance of the external environment. Reviewing several possible environmental information subsystems (e.g., competitive information, regulatory information, image information), these authors stress that such subsystems should be integrated in terms of their output, which "must be compatible and available in the aggregate for use in decision problem analysis if new and more sophisticated varieties of information systems are to lead to more effective strategic decision making."[18]

Environmental Forecasting Techniques

The Utterback study identified four major approaches to forecasting: "quantification of expert opinion"; extrapolation of trends; monitoring or scanning the environment; and simulation of the interaction of environmental variables.[19] The best known example of quantifying expert opinion is the Delphi method, which involves a panel of experts reaching formal consensus on the probability of future occurrences within particular time frames. The publication of numerous articles describing the method and its applications has helped to make it perhaps the most popular of the more qualitative techniques. It has recently been seriously criticized for its reportedly unscientific, unreliable approach, and Utterback notes that the "popularity of the approach has resulted in many poorly designed and inappropriate studies."[20]

Utterback points out that extrapolation of trends was

one of the earliest methods of forecasting technological change, using equations based both on empirical and theoretical results to develop projections from available data. Monitoring "involves searching the environment for signals that may be the forerunner of significant change, identifying the possible consequences—assuming that the indications persist—and choosing the events and decisions that should be observed and followed in order to verify the speed and timing of the anticipated change. This method is predicated on the idea that change will be visible in increasingly tangible forms over a period of time before it assumes economic, social or strategic importance."[21]

Although one author reports that almost 2,000 North American firms are using, developing, or experimenting with some kind of computer-based corporate planning model, Utterback notes that the use of simulation in forecasting has been largely an "exploratory" effort because of problems with measurement and the difficulty of understanding underlying relationships. He points out that two aspects of simulation merit special attention: the simplification of relationships and the level of aggregation of relationships used in the development of a model.[22]

At its broadest, the so-called "futures" field refers to the formulation of one or more future scenarios, or sets of events likely to occur in the future. In a 1978 report, the Conference Board noted that scenario planning had emerged in the 1970s in response to tremendous environmental uncertainty, but that it was seldom formally implemented. Executives responding to the Conference Board's survey indicated that three basic scenarios appeared the "most practical to work with": most probable, pessimistic, and optimistic.[23] It appears that, in practice, scenario building has been largely a qualitative endeavor, reflecting the belief that policy decisions are primarily judgmental in nature. It is acknowledged, however, that broad qualitative scenarios are most effective when used in conjunction with narrower, more quantitative forecasts; indeed, in the process of working through scenarios, planners can pinpoint where quantitative approaches are needed.

Many of the large-scale firms that have implemented strategic planning take a multifaceted approach to forecasting, combining both quantitative and qualitative techniques. The Monsanto Company, for example, has reported that it employs three types of forecasting as part of its long-range corporate planning: trend analysis, expert opinion, and normative forecasting. The firm does not utilize the formal Delphi technique because of its "rigidity" and time-consuming nature; instead, an expert is presented with a scenario or set of factors or projections, and asked to comment. The normative approach is intended to paint a picture of what the firm wants the future to be, as a means of identifying where actions are required to realize the desired scenario.[24]

General Electric is well known for the breadth and depth of its environmental forecasting, which is characterized by "grinding, step-by-step" analysis. To quote a senior executive of the firm: "When we look at the external environment . . . we consider how social, economic, political and technological trends have in the past, and will in the future, impact our markets, customers, competitors, industries and suppliers. From this we derive opportunities and threats."[25] The firm is careful to avoid over-reliance on computer-driven models and quantitative analysis, assuring that forecasts draw on the judgments of experienced managers.[26]

The Bell System Emerging Issues Program is impressive in both the extent of participation in its forecasting process and the scope of the analysis. The program was developed in response to the need for "consistent, systematic analyses of external issues and trends and a mechanism by which to determine which of those myriad issues on the horizon scarce management time and corporate resources should be devoted to." Bell's top management recognized the need to be well informed on the "soft" issues such as consumerism and attitudes toward technology, as well as on the more traditional "hard" areas, such as economic trends.

The Bell System's Corporate Issues Group, with staff support from the corporate planning unit, was formed to act as a "think tank and consulting group," responsible for providing leadership and coordination in the formulation of an annual forecasts and assumptions document. This document is distributed company-wide, before detailed planning guidelines are written, as the "basic presuppositions about the environment in which we will be doing business." Even before the creation of the forecasts and assumptions document, the Group, with staff support, draws up a list of significant topics. A definition and projection are prepared for each issue or topic, and this preliminary paper is widely distributed for comment and modification. Eventually each topic has an ad hoc interdepartmental committee formed around it. These committees develop issue papers, which are compiled and edited into the forecasts and assumptions document.[27]

Broad Guidelines

The following factors should be taken into consideration in designing an environmental scanning process:

☐ The complexity and turbulence or unpredictability of an organization's environment will most likely be the primary determinant of the degree of formality and sophistication of its forecasting system. In other words, the more stable the environment and the fewer the relevant environmental variables to be analyzed, the simpler and more informal the system required.

☐ The exercise of disciplined and trained perception and intuition should never be subordinated to quantitative methods. It is essential that a balance be maintained, not only between the quantitative and qualitative, but also between the formal and informal approaches. The point is to ensure that as many perspectives as feasible are brought to bear on the forecasting problem, and that formality not be allowed to narrow the focus prematurely, thus filtering out potentially significant, if currently faint, "signals" from the environment.

☐ Closely related to the foregoing point is the requirement that an organization provide its managers with education and training aimed at enhancing their perception and intuition, in addition to practical opportunities to test these capabilities. Although some people may be born with a stronger creative or intuitive capability than others, there is no question that one can learn to be more perceptive, to distinguish a greater number of variables, and to discern patterns among variables not previously recognized. Therefore, the development of an organization's human resources can be at least as important, if not more so, as an investment in technology.

☐ No matter how well designed the forecasting process, its ultimate utility will depend most on how carefully it is integrated into the overall strategic planning and management process. The planning system design will preferably address in specific terms how the products of the forecasting process will be used in formulating strategies.

☐ Finally, the wider the scope and greater the depth of the forecasting process, the more expensive it is likely to be in terms of staff time and technology, especially when computer support is required to any extent. The additional cost required to collect and analyze a larger volume of data may be justified by the results, but such ramifications should be carefully considered during the design stage.

3. The Internal Resource Audit

The basic purpose of the resource audit step in the strategic planning process is to assess the internal strengths and weaknesses of an organization, along as many dimensions as appear to have relevance to the implementation of the current or new strategic directions. Of course, resource strengths and weaknesses are relative; they have meaning only in the context of particular strategies and specific environmental opportunities and constraints. Certain strategic directions will call for sophisticated production technology, a strong research and development capability, or a highly flexible, innovative, and aggressive general management—or all of these at one time. The obvious objective is to assure that the organization can support the strategies which it has selected, either within its current resource capability or through building the resources needed.

Professor Ansoff has explored this question in his examination of what he calls an organization's "strategic capability," which is "a measure of effectiveness of an ESO (environment-serving organization) in supporting a particular (strategic) thrust." Ansoff has identified three resource components that, taken together, determine the strategic capacity of an organization: general management, which provides overall leadership to an organization; "logistic" management, which is responsible for implementing the strategic thrust by constructing facilities, developing products, organizing production, marketing, and distribution processes, and other functions; and the range and quality of the technology at the organization's command. An organization's strategic capability is "optimal" when

> all competence components match the strategic thrust, when the capacity is adequately matched to the strategic budget, and when the technology is the best available for meeting the demands of the market place.[28]

Professor Uyterhoeven and his colleagues have identified three main dimensions of the resource audit: the operational, the financial, and the managerial. The operational dimension consists of the functions and processes involved in producing the services or products of the firm and in seeing that they reach the consumer. What is produced, and what technology is involved? To what degree are such functions as research and development, marketing, and distribution developed? In addition, given the current strategic thrust of the organization, what are the principal criteria of success or effectiveness for each operational function? In other words, what environmental opportunities and constraints have dictated the scope and depth of each function?

The financial dimension is concerned with understanding the financial condition of an organization and the dynamics of its financing. What are the current uses of the organization's resources (e.g., working capital, fixed assets, investments) and where have they been generated (e.g., debt, equity)? What does its balance sheet look like? What are its asset requirements per dollar of sales? What do its earnings look like as compared to sales, equity, assets?

The managerial dimension covers two areas: human resources and management systems, including policies and procedures. Noting that this dimension is "probably the most critical," Uyterhoeven observes that it is also in many respects the most difficult to evaluate. In assessing the human dimension, the organization would identify the competence of its management in various categories, including general management (strategic leadership, executive management), operational management (the "line" at different levels, from foreman up), staff or technical management (planners, research and development staff, personnel managers, budget analysts, and the like). It would also be critical to assess the nonmanagerial workforce in terms of its skills level and other less tangible characteristics (morale, work habits, commitment, to name a few of the more important).

Far more subjective but no less important than the categorization of the firm's management is the need to identify those characteristics that can enhance or impede the implementation of strategies to understand the firm's "mentality" and "culture." For example, what are the attitudes and practices regarding risk-taking, innovation, flexibility? What are the values and expectations which govern managerial behavior? Is there a tradition of bringing executives through the ranks over a long period, or is "new blood" regularly infused into the organization at the top? Is the prevailing style laissez-faire, or is the atmosphere authoritarian? What is the ethical framework within which plans and action must fit? The point is to paint as detailed a picture of the human side of the organization as possible in order to pinpoint the relevant constraints, weaknesses, and strengths.

The canvas is not finished until the management support infrastructure is detailed. It is important to understand the strengths and weaknesses of such support systems as planning, budgeting, auditing, accounting, computer services, research, and evaluation. Is there a formal policies and procedures system; how are those policies and procedures communicated, maintained, and updated; and what subject matter is covered? Is there a management information system? What technology supports the information system; what reports are issued to which managers and how frequently?[29]

In summary, it behooves the organization that is contemplating new strategic directions to know itself thoroughly, and the more dramatic the break with the past, the more detailed the knowledge should be. It is important to determine what gaps exist between the resources needed to pursue a new strategy and those currently possessed by the organization. Is it feasible in terms of time and money to build the required resource base, or is the cost such that it would make more sense to alter the strategy itself? To ignore these questions is to increase the risk of failure as the strategic plan is implemented.

4. The Formulation, Evaluation, and Selection of Strategies

At this stage in the strategic planning process, the organization has documented its strategic profile, formulated an environmental forecast, and taken stock of its internal resources. Given its understanding of environmental opportunities and constraints and its internal strengths and weaknesses, the organization is in a position to generate alternative strategies to take maximum feasible advantage of its existing and potential strengths and the opportunities that have been identified. There is substantial opinion favoring a relatively unrestrained process of generating strategic options, with the understanding that essential discipline will be imposed during the assessment and selection phases. Uyterhoeven, for one, urges a freely creative process in order to assure that sound, high opportunity options are not prematurely filtered out only because of their unconventionality. To his way of thinking, the process should accommodate "unconventional or even crazy ideas" since the evaluation process is very likely to ensure that "the bad ones will be weeded out and the occasional good ones retained for future exploration."[30]

There is no *one* structural or procedural model for the process of formulating strategy. As is true for the overall strategic planning process and the internal and external environmental analysis stages, the elaborateness and formality of the formulation process depend on the unique circumstances of the given organization. Lorange and Vancil have set forth a formal three-cycle strategy formulation process for the large diversified corporation, consisting of corporate, business and functional planning, and strategy formulation. At the opposite pole, a smaller company might require only periodic meetings of the chief executive with his or her key executives to map out strategies, without employing any more elaborate or formal process.[31]

In the case of a large, multidivisional firm with a variety of kinds of strategies at different levels of detail (e.g., corporate, business), the question of integration becomes important, whether or not a comprehensive planning document is assembled. At the least, the firm will want to determine that the various plans are mutually supportive and that major contradictions do not occur. It would not be appropriate in this introductory treatment of the subject to explore structural approaches to achieving such integration; suffice it so say that in such complex settings a highly formal, structured process is most likely in order.

Generation of Options

The strategic planner can call upon a wide variety of techniques for generating and analyzing strategic options; the choice of specific techniques will depend on the complexity of the external environment, the aspirations of the organization (Is there a strong drive to innovate, to diversify?), and the resources available to invest in the strategic formulation process. The general consensus appears to favor a mix of qualitative and analytical techniques, with the former approach weighing more heavily in the generation of options and the latter in the evaluation phase. An especially noteworthy advance has been the development of strategy assessment processes closely tied to resource allocation, the best-known probably being General Electric's "business screen."

At the least constrained end of the spectrum of approaches is brainstorming, which the literature indicates is used by most large corporations early in the strategic planning process as a means of generating a variety of new ideas. More rigorous but still heavily qualitative in approach is the development of detailed scenarios, which either "describe in detail a sequence of events which could plausibly lead to a prescribed end state" or "consider the possible outcomes of present choices." Although largely qualitative, scenarios are often quite detailed and have the advantage of considering in an integrated fashion several diverse factors. Another basically qualitative approach is Policy Delphi, which was briefly reviewed in our discussion of environmental forecasting. It is a means of refining analyses resulting from the comparison of alternative scenarios. "In situations where no single optimal solution can be found, the Policy Delphi seeks to explore opposing personal interpretations of data by developing the strongest possible opposite points of view on policy issues."[32]

Channon attributes the rapid growth in techniques for generating and evaluating strategic options to the pressure of rapid and discontinuous environmental change. He points out that managers are increasingly planning under a "series of alternative future environmental scenarios," which may include "built-in trigger points which call into action predetermined contingency plans." One facet of this development is the increasing attention to less quantifiable socio-political variables, which more and more often are being factored into models for strategic assessment.[33]

Portfolio Techniques

To Channon, the most important development in techniques for tying strategy assessment to resource allocation is the adoption of corporate portfolio techniques, which means that resources are "increasingly being allocated according to a corporate strategic perspective of each business within the total portfolio." The models are, in his estimation, "the first major advances in systematically identifying the main underlying, strategic characteristics of special individual businesses. . . ."[34] A variety of portfolio models have been designed and tested in practice over the past few years, and four will be briefly discussed: the growth/share matrix; the business assessment array (or business planning matrix); the directional policy matrix; and the PIMS (Profit Impact of Marketing Strategy) Program of the Strategic Planning Institute.

A recent study of portfolio models suggests that there are three major ways in which the models can differ conceptually: whether the model provides a general prescriptive framework or is more closely tailored to the specific circumstances of the organization using it; the dimensions used in developing the model; and the degree to which rules for allocating resources are imposed. The authors set forth seven steps involved in analyzing a portfolio:

☐ Determining the level and unit of analysis and the links connecting them.
☐ Identifying both the single-variable and composite dimensions.
☐ Establishing the relative importance of the dimensions.
☐ Constructing a matrix based on two or more dominant dimensions.
☐ Positioning products or businesses in the matrix.
☐ Projecting the probable position of each product or business given (1) no significant changes in the external environmental conditions, competitive situation, or established strategies and (2) expected changes in any of these factors.
☐ Choosing the desired position for each current or new product and business ("as a basis for developing alternative strategies to close the gap between the current and new portfolios") and determining the most effective allocation of resources among the businesses and products.[35]

Growth/Share Matrix The earliest and most simplistic of the portfolio models is the growth/share bivariate matrix developed by the Boston Consulting Group (BCG). The model is based on the "experience curve" concept— that when the accumulative manufacturing experience of a product doubles, the total cost per unit tends to decrease by 20 to 30 percent in real terms. The highest profits should thus accrue to the competitor with the highest market share or relative competitive dominance because its costs would be lowest. "Using the experience curve concept, therefore, the most successful competitive strategy is to achieve and hold a dominant market position either through pricing tactics or by segmenting the market into discrete sectors which can be dominated and defended." If market dominance cannot be obtained, then, it is argued, an orderly withdrawal may represent the optimal strategy.

Products or businesses can be positioned on the matrix as:

- ☐ "Stars." — high market share, high growth potential.
- ☐ "Cash cows" — high market share, low growth potential.
- ☐ "Wildcats" — low market share, high growth.
- ☐ "Dogs" — low market share, low growth.

The model has been criticized as conceptually questionable in light of its forcing the comparison into two variables and for its lack of guidance in determining the appropriate mix of stars, dogs, wildcats and cash cows, with the exception of balance of cash flows.[36]

Business Assessment Array The business assessment array or business planning matrix, developed by McKinsey and Company and General Electric, is more sophisticated than the growth/share matrix in that it utilizes a nine-cell matrix in attempting to relate two composite variables: a firm's strengths and industry attractiveness. The former variable consists of such factors as human resources, market share, financial condition, and technology. The latter includes growth rate, profitability, technology, labor market, and competitive structure, among other fac-

FIGURE 5

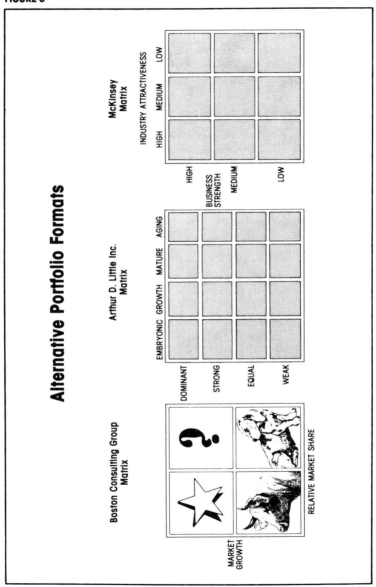

Alternative Portfolio Formats

Boston Consulting Group Matrix

Arthur D. Little Inc. Matrix

McKinsey Matrix

tors. One assessment of the model concludes that, despite the lack of "rigorous" research supporting the model, "the fact that some of the most sophisticated industrial and consulting firms subscribe to the basic outline strongly suggests that it provides a comfortable mix of quantitative and qualitative elements which have been found to be useful in practice."[37]

Directional Policy Matrix   The directional policy matrix, developed by the Dutch Royal Shell Group in collaboration with a major consulting firm, utilizes a nine-cell matrix with two composite dimensions: sector profitability and competitive position within the segment. As with the business assessment array, this approach has the advantage of introducing greater complexity than the growth/share matrix, but the disadvantage of losing some of its rigor in terms of quantification.[38]

PIMS   Building on a data base of the experience of over 1500 companies, the PIMS Program of the Strategic Planning Institute offers, according to Derek Channon, "perhaps the most important single strategic decision making tool" that has been developed. PIMS consists of several models that, among other results, have enabled us to understand the impact of nine strategic variables on a firm's profitability, including productivity, market growth, market position, investment intensity, innovation, and vertical integration. Although Allio and Pennington observe that PIMS findings for the most part "do nothing more than confirm conventional wisdom," they consider it a "major advance" in strategic planning because of the empirical validation and quantification of the variables.[39]

Caveat Emptor:
Use with Discretion

Although the efficacy of portfolio models in strategy formulation is widely acknowledged, the general caveats applying to any analytical technique should be kept in mind. No model is a panacea, answering all questions; the need for human judgment, intuition, and creativity are just as great, if not greater. Any approach involves costs, as well as benefits, and the user will want to consider whether the latter justify the former. In general, one is well advised to proceed with discretion and caution. In their recent examination of portfolio models, Wind and Mahajan caution that the models are useful primarily for analysis of the relationships among products and business units and that they do not answer such questions as when to milk a cash cow or dispose of a dog. The portfolio approach is useful for analysis and evaluation of strategic options, they point out, only when it "exploits management's creativity and imagination—instead of conforming to some general prescription." They further observe that:

☐ It is important to understand particular portfolio models in enough depth to recognize their limitations. For example, when dealing with composite-dimension models, such as the business assessment array and the directional policy matrix, the user should keep in mind that: (1) important differences among products may be masked; (2) the process of establishing relationships involves subjective evaluations that may differ, raising questions as to how to reach consensus; and (3) the weighting system may not take into account close correlations among factors, thus producing a misleading product classification.

☐ Although the 2 x 2 or 3 x 3 matrix is attractive because of its simplicity, it can be misleading if important dimensions and the conditions under which a recommended strategy is likely to be effective are ignored.

☐ A portfolio approach tailored to a particular firm is likely to be most effective in strategy formulation, but will cost more in terms of data requirements and management time.[40]

Despite the availability of increasingly more sophisticated analytical tools to assist in formulating and assessing strategies, in the final analysis evaluating and choosing among alternative strategies is a highly complex and judgmental activity. As Uyterhoeven observes, the process is too often erroneously described as purely logical and capable of obtaining the best of all worlds. In practice, of course, one does not maximize opportunities and minimize constraints; one accepts manageable levels of risk and constraints along with less than full realization of opportunities. In short, one engages in the normal compromise and trading-off that characterizes so much of the management job.[41]

Evaluation of Options

The basic questions which must be asked in assessing particular strategies fall for the most part into three broad categories: (1) strategy formulation process design; (2) content of particular strategies; and (3) implementation factors. The theoretical and applied literature on strategic planning is sufficient to provide certain reasonably reliable criteria for assessing strategy formulation processes, even though such assessment must obviously be tailored to specific organizational and environmental situations. Granted the assessment will be rather rough, but better that than no attempt to evaluate the formulation process. For example, certain questions should be raised if no attempt is made to supplement qualitative formulation approaches with one or more of the widely used analytical techniques, or if there is no senior management participation in the process beyond the chief executive and his immediate office staff.

There are likewise certain obvious questions which can be asked in the area of implementation. Does the organization possess, or can it acquire, the necessary resources? Is the internal political climate favorable, or at least manageable, and are key staff committed to the strategy? Is the organizational structure adequate to support the strategy?[42]

Steiner and Miner have suggested several questions relative to the content of a strategy:

☐ Does it conform with the mission of the organization?
☐ Is it consistent with the organization's external environment?
☐ Is the strategy consistent with the organization's in-

ternal strengths, policies, and value system?
☐ Does it provide an acceptable balance between risk and profit potential?
☐ Does it make sense in terms of the competitive situation?
☐ Is it consistent with other strategies in the company, or at least not in major conflict?
☐ Is the strategy complete, in that it consists of substrategies that interrelate properly, the identification of required resources, and implementation plans?
☐ Is its timing correct?[43]

5. Strategy Implementation

Thousands upon thousands of feet of shelf space may be devoted to housing the typical long-range plan, which is soon forgotten and little if ever referred to, its sole eternal purpose to gather dust along with its millions of useless shelfmates. Hyperbole? No experienced manager would be likely to take exception to this grim description of the afterlife in store for even the best conceived and intended long-range planning document. Why are the products of so much precious human time and energy consigned so often to oblivion? The reason is relatively simple: very little time and thought are devoted to implementing plans. To many managers, the planning document is an end in itself, its mission accomplished with its commitment to paper.

Now, there are various reasons for giving short shrift to what is a highly important, complex, and demanding dimension of the strategic management process, a dimension that should claim considerable managerial attention. It is safe to assume that malevolence is rarely encountered in the world of planning and that the great majority of planners would be aghast at the thought of consciously designing a planning process, or producing a plan, in order to see it fail. More likely what is at work is a lack of understanding of the dynamics of the implementation, perhaps along with very human desires to avoid pain and suffering and to realize the proverbial "something for nothing."

Whatever the reasons for paying inadequate attention

to the implementation process, the result is all too often failure. Experience teaches that if proper attention is given to implementation, the success rate in achieving planned goals and objectives is increased significantly. Five facets of implementation are addressed: (1) the role of the chief executive; (2) organization structure; (3) the tie to operations; (4) managerial support and commitment; and (5) the implementation plan.

No attempt has been made to deal separately with the two closely related aspects of implementation—the planning *process*, and the resulting *plans*—because the factors influencing successful implementation are for the most part common to both aspects. It is obvious that the planning process and plan are intertwined: how the process is implemented impacts not only the quality of the resulting plans, but also the means for carrying out those plans. This is to say that even if a poorly executed process generates planning products of potential positive value to an organization, it is likely to be very difficult to realize this value, in large measure because of the loss of credibility of the lacking reinforcement.

The Chief Executive's Role

To many students of management, strategic thinking, planning, and decision making are the primary responsibility of an organization's chief executive officer. Few would question that the chief executive is an organization's preeminent strategist, that his or her active support is an essential element in successful strategic planning, and that even his or her neutrality, much less opposition, is enough to cripple the planning process. To Steiner, there "can and will be no effective comprehensive corporate planning in any organization where the chief executive does not give it firm support and make sure that others in the organization understand his depth of commitment." This role, he observes, is neither as obvious as it should be, nor very clearly understood.[44]

Ansoff sees strategic leadership as a three-fold function: "to conceive the vision, to communicate and inspire others with the vision, and to influence the firm to follow the vision." Ansoff's "vision" consists of the common purposes of an organization and the means to achieve them. The strategic leadership role encompasses three sub-roles:

- ☐ "Legitimizing leadership," which involves defining the purpose of the organization and the criteria for its success;
- ☐ "Decision leadership," which involves making strategic choices; and
- ☐ "Action leadership," which is concerned with implementation of strategic plans.[45]

Ansoff's action leadership, which includes maintaining a climate supportive of the plan, mobilizing management participation in strategic planning, generating support for implementation, and coordinating and controlling implementation, is different from, though very closely related to, his decision leadership. They require different tasks and call for different skills and talents. Decision leadership calls for intellectual, analytical, and creative skills, while action leadership entails the mobilization, organization, and motivation of human energies to carry out strategic directions. "Action leadership assures the will to solve difficult and unpleasant problems, and decision leadership assures that they are solved creatively."[46]

Andrews's view of the three-fold strategic role of the chief executive is almost identical to Ansoff's. As the "architect" of strategy, the chief executive takes the lead in developing the strategic plan for the organization. As the "implementer" of strategy, he or she mobilizes and directs the organization's resources in carrying out the plan. As the "personal leader," the chief executive, through his personal leadership style, ideals, visions, and behavior, sets the overall tone and expectations for the organization.[47]

As pointed out in a Conference Board report on the role of the chief executive in planning, the top officer's climate-setting responsibility involves assuming at times the educator and evangelist roles, explaining and selling long-range planning by word and by deed.[48] Now, there is no doubt that the word is important, especially when it issues from the chief executive. It is useful to read what the chief executive has to say about the planning process, its purposes and procedures, and it can be inspiring to hear the organization's leader articulate his or her vision of what the firm can and should aspire to become. But that hackneyed phrase "actions speak louder than words" is nowhere so true as in the area of long-range planning. Written pronouncements seldom cause more than a ripple in the waters of a large organization. When the object of attention is planning, the inbuilt resistance and pressures working against it, which tend to intensify as the time frame of planning lengthens, mean that mere words, be they instructional or exhortatory, are unlikely to influence behavior in any significant way.

The denizens of large-scale organizations have developed very sensitive antennae over the course of human evolution. Their senses are particularly acute when it comes to spotting discrepancies between word and deed. They have learned to pay only slight attention to the directions that reach them via interoffice memorandums; they adopt a policy of watchful waiting, deferring judgment until actions either clearly support and confirm the written word or clearly contradict, and hence nullify, what they have read. The absence of action tends to have the effect of nullification. The reader may have worked in an organization headed by a chief executive who kicked off the strategic planning process with exhortations of the most forceful variety, but who quickly became conspicuous by his or her absence during the course of planning, who could find little if any time for planning and plan review sessions. Through such contradictory actions is the credibility of long-range planning eroded.

The constant reinforcement of the importance of long-range planning is a critical factor in maintaining a positive climate for planning and implementation. The most important aspect of this reinforcement is the visible, active involvement of the chief executive in activities aimed at implementing strategic directions. Regular progress reviews, involving the chief executive's sustained, personal participation, would be a powerful confirmation of the importance of the plan in the hierarchy of organizational priorities. Implementation also requires that the chief executive must both make and implement a variety of decisions; acting in a timely fashion on these matters, including resource allocations and alterations in the organizational structure, cannot help but strengthen the place of the strategic plan.

It is the overall responsibility of the chief executive to assure that all of the elements key to the success of the organization's strategic plan are in place. The requisite resources must be allocated to strategic programs. The necessary staffing, organizational structure, policies and procedures, and support systems must be present. A suitable management information system should be in place to enable regular monitoring of implementation. These and other facets of implementation, which are addressed in greater detail later in this book, are the overall responsibility of the chief executive.

Steiner observes that two major barriers to chief executives' ability to effectively carry out their strategic responsibilities are the scarcity of time and the chief executive's own temperament. The claims on the chief executive's time are, of course, numerous, and there will be constant pressure to attend to short-term matters at the expense of the more strategic concerns. Remarkable self-discipline and commitment to the idea of strategic planning are required to preserve time for strategic planning matters. The temperament of a chief executive is frequently shaped in highly action-oriented functional jobs, with rewards being based on short-term successes. The change in focus required in strategic management can be radical.[49]

Organization Structure

Two basic structural questions are involved in strategic planning: the appropriate organization for planning and the organization best suited to implementation of strategies. With regard to the planning process, it is critical to determine whether the existing organization used for management and control purposes is sufficient to do the planning which must be done. The people will not change—managers plan, not the "planners"—but they may need to be grouped differently to do planning. There is large-scale experience in designing and successfully implementing planning organizations not congruent with the management structure, such as General Electric's Strategic Business Units. King and Cleland make a convincing case for the use of such a special planning structure, describing it as a "continuous, parallel, ongoing organization that complements the basic operating organization."

> It operates with a different pattern of authorities and responsibilities than exist in the operating organization. This is so because it has different objectives than does the operating organization and because different people may have the knowledge and expertise necessary for leadership in such an environment.[50]

Not every organization would want to attempt to create a separate planning structure: some would be too small to handle the complexity; others may have too weak a planning foundation to support and fully utilize such an elaborate approach. There are certainly alternatives involving less elaborate structure, such as the use of task forces crossing organizational lines at appropriate points in the planning process. It is widely agreed that any fair-sized organization does need a special planning office, responsible for designing, coordinating, and supporting the planning process, and this question is dealt with later in the book.

The thesis that organizational structure generally follows an organization's strategy, its specific design features taking shape in response to the requirement to support the strategic directions of the organization, has become so firmly ensconced in conventional management wisdom that it is easy to forget that the first full-blown exposition was in Alfred Chandler's 1962 study, *Strategy and Structure.* Chandler, a highly respected business historian, based his thesis on substantial empirical research in American corporate history. He defines structure as "the design of the organization through which the enterprise is administered," and includes two aspects of the design:

lines of authority and communication, and the information and data flowing along these lines. His basic thesis is that when an organization changes its strategy in response to environmental changes, the mismatch between the new strategy and old structure causes economic inefficiency that, when it grows serious enough to be recognized, forces structural redesign in order to restore efficiency.[51]

The basic Chandlerian thesis has proved quite durable over nearly twenty years, but subsequent research has elaborated and enriched the main theme. Two of the more prominent students of the strategy-structure connection, Galbraith and Nathanson, have contributed important elaborations, among them that:

☐ Structure not only follows strategy, but it also plays an important role in shaping strategy.

☐ Organizations appear to be able to live with the mismatch between structure and strategy, with its concomitant economic inefficiency, to the extent that competition is not present to supply pressure to restructure.

☐ Facets other than structure that must be considered when dealing with organization are (1) resource allocation processes; (2) evaluation and reward systems; and (3) people and careers. A "congruence between people, rewards, information and decision processes and structure is needed to effectively implement a given strategy."[52]

Andrews sets forth general guidance for approaching the structural design question, the starting point of which is the identification of strategic tasks to be performed in the implementation plan, assignment of responsibility for performance, and the allocation of the authority required to do and to see that the tasks are done. Depending on the nature of the strategies set forth in the plan, there are a variety of approaches to organizational structure, or combinations thereof, including the functional, geographical, market, and product. Generally speaking, he advises that the structure be no more complex than absolutely required and that it be as flexible as possible. He also suggests that designers avoid "typical" organizational patterns whose only attraction is apparent widespread use; each organization is unique in terms of its internal resources and its strategic requirements, and this calls for a tailoring of the structure to the specific situation.[53]

Although reorganization can be a powerful tool for realigning resources, human and material, it can also introduce massive short-term inefficiencies. It is wise, therefore, to err on the conservative side, disrupting established patterns only to the extent absolutely required to ensure timely and cost-effective achievement of strategic goals and objectives.

When considering how to structure an organization in order to pursue strategic objectives, there is more involved than the configuration of organizational units and lines of authority and communication. As has already been noted, it is crucial to establish that the management capability is adequate to undertake implementation efforts. For example, if implementation progress is to be monitored on a regular basis, there must be some kind of management information system capable of collecting the pertinent financial and other data and reporting it in usable form. A large, multidivisional firm will most likely require several different monitoring reports, taking several "cuts" on the data and providing various levels of aggregation depending on the particular audience. To build such a system when little or no foundation exists can be extremely time consuming and expensive, especially if large-scale computer support is necessary (and it usually is essential to handle many data elements). Another important facet of the infrastructure is the personnel management system, particularly those components dealing with management evaluation, compensation, and other incentives. This is discussed in some detail later in this book, but it should be kept in mind that nothing is likely to be more influential in securing management commitment and support for new initiatives, especially when they are at all threatening, than the compensation system.

The Linkage to Operational Planning

There is significant support in the literature for the

establishment of ties between the strategic plan and planning process and the annual operating plan and budget. The obvious connection is the annual allocation of resources to those commitments of the strategic plan that fall due each year. No linkage at all between the strategic plan and annual planning and resource allocation would certainly signal a lack of seriousness in the strategic planning process, thus damaging its credibility. Beyond multiyear resource allocation, which must of necessity be only tentative in large part, there should, many believe, be an annual "fallout," an explicit tie between the strategic plan and annual budget. According to this view, the first (or current) year of a five-year plan would be developed in considerably greater detail in the course of the annual budget process. To Steiner, budgeting bridges "the gap between strategic planning and current actions," and not only facilitates "but forces integration of functional elements in both the development of plans and in carrying them out."[54]

The authors of a relatively recent article focusing on the frequent gaps between the strategic plan and the operating plans on which its ultimate implementation depends, suggest five ways to ensure that the requisite "coupling" of strategic and operating plans takes place":

☐ Guarding against the generation of strategic goals that force impossible operating goals;

☐ Segregating serious operational changes dictated by a new strategy so that the total operation is not disrupted;

☐ Paying explicit attention to the solution of coupling issues;

☐ Making certain that strategic plans explicitly identify follow-through operational steps and impacts; and

☐ Promoting wide and clear understanding of the strategic plan.[55]

A 1973 study draws on the experience of six successful firms in examining the balance between creativity and practicality in planning. The authors are convinced that the major means for the enhancement of "realism" in planning is to give it a "clear action orientation," primarily through the creation of a close tie between long-range planning and annual budget control. The potential serious defect in this approach to grounding planning in reality is the promotion of a focus "that can be disastrous to mind-stretching reach." There is no golden rule for striking the right balance, which will change as the organization's circumstances change, but that must be maintained if the organization is to cope with change. The authors suggest that the necessary linkage can take three forms: through content, utilizing the same basic data for long-range planning and budgeting; through organization, relating the units handling planning and budgeting coordination; and through process, basically tying the two processes together through chronological sequencing.[56]

Steiner and Miner, pointing out that linking the strategic plan to the annual budget is the "most universally used and central basis for translating strategic decisions into current actions," suggest that other techniques can be useful in this regard, including the network of policies and procedures, Management by Objectives (MBO), such scheduling models as Performance Evaluation Review Techniques (PERT), and an organization's communication system. With regard to the degree of coordination between strategic and annual operating plans, the authors observe that detailed coordination would be cumbersome, complex, and "extremely difficult," especially in large and diverse organizations. Their advice is to provide highly selective coordination, focusing only on those plan elements essential to the accomplishment of strategic aims.[57]

Not only would an attempt to integrate and coordinate strategic and operational planning and budgeting in detail pose serious, perhaps overwhelming, technical and logistical problems, it would also be conceptually suspect. In light of the accelerating rate of environmental change and the increase in environmental complexity—forcing organizations to identify, track, and forecast not only more variables, but also variables changing more rapidly—the need for greater flexibility in the strategic planning process is obvious. Response time is necessarily decreasing, and strategies are constantly being reexamined and altered more frequently. This situation argues for relatively few formal ties between the two plans and planning processes, basically only those essential to the full and timely implementation of strategies. Never should the coordination process become so complex that it impedes strategic planning and decision making.

Managerial Support and Commitment

As was observed before, the "human factor" is most likely the most complex and important element in designing and implementing strategic planning systems and carrying out strategies. Experience points the finger at the human dimension, far more than the technological, in assigning responsibility for implementation failures. How much simpler the task of the strategic planner and decision maker if he or she had only to attend to technical and structural design questions!

There are surely hundreds of ways for managers to impede the implementation of strategies, without having to indulge in open hostility or frontal assault. And the larger the bureaucracy and more complex the strategies, the more opportunities there are for creative opposition. Any chief executive officer with a commitment to strategic planning, therefore, is well advised to factor explicitly into the organization's strategic implementation plan the human dimension and to accord it high priority. Given the commitment and skill, people have been known to neutralize and even overcome technical system design flaws, but systems are not renowned for compensating for human shortcomings.

This discussion of the human dimension in implementation of the strategic plan will focus on four facets of the question of building managerial support and commitment:

- ☐ Through inspiration, education, and general communication.
- ☐ Through meaningful participation.
- ☐ Through specific internal process or system features.
- ☐ Through a proper match between the person and the job.

In our discussion of the role of the chief executive in implementing the plan, we pointed out his preeminent responsibility for communicating the purposes and substance of the organization's strategies in such a manner that they could be understood by all managers. We also mentioned the chief executive's responsibility for inspiring and educating his or her managers to accept the importance of the longer perspective provided through strategic planning. Granted, this alone is quite unlikely to build the requisite support and active commitment, but it is an important starting point. In his review of the elements involved in the successful implementation of change, Warren Bennis affirms the critical role of communication, not only to promote cognitive understanding, but also emotional commitment.[58] Sir Geoffrey Vickers avers that communication can change what he terms the "appreciative system" of managers—their ability to perceive and to evaluate environmental features.[59]

There is no question that participation in the formulation of strategies builds managerial commitment and support for carrying them out, so long as such participation is "meaningful" in the sense that it truly does help to shape the ultimate strategies. Ritualistic participation, aimed only at creating a facade of participation, is far more likely to backfire, resulting in serious opposition to the plan. There is, therefore, a need to design the participatory process carefully, ensuring that the people participating at any stage do, indeed, have a real contribution to make.[60] There are certainly numerous examples of large organizations that involve many managers at different levels in what appear to be effective strategic planning processes. General Electric and the Bell System are two of the more notable organizations mentioned in this study. Such firms believe that their strategic plans benefit from the different perspectives and experiential and knowledge bases brought to the process by managers involved in a wide range of functions, businesses, and levels of management.

One planning scholar suggests that management by objectives (MBO)—which basically involves a manager's reaching agreement with his or her immediate superior, relative to the specific objectives to be pursued and used in evaluating performance—is a useful device for realizing participation in development of the implementation plan.[61] This may indeed be an especially "meaningful" approach to participation in light of its proximity to a manager's day-to-day world, requiring that those aspects of the strategic plan "falling due" during the upcoming budget year be factored into the manager's objectives statement.

There is no question that attempts to strengthen the strategic frame of reference of an organization's managers, and to build their commitment and support for new strategies, are frequently in fundamental conflict with strong, at times overwhelming, pressure for short-term results. The successful manager necessarily understands and responds to the reward system of an organization, and what is done in practice decides behavior, not what is said. As Andrews has observed, since managers respond to the "measures management actually takes to reward performance, mere verbal exhortations to behave in the manner required by long-range strategy carry no weight, and cannot be relied upon to preclude undesirable actions encouraged by a poorly designed measurement and reward system."[62] There are likely many organizations in which pervasive pressure to produce larger current profits, a course of action often at variance with one or more strategic aims, leads to this fundamentally dishonest scenario: the leader extolls the virtues of strategic planning and decision making and afterwards punishes and rewards managers solely on the basis of short-term performance.

If the chief executive is seriously committed to strategic planning and management, there are a variety of techniques available to assist in countering the shorter-term pressures. Banks and Wheelwright have, for example, isolated certain factors that often strengthen short-run concerns at the expense of strategic ones, including the performance measurement system, internal communications, and operational gaps between annual and long-range planning. The authors recommend that balance be promoted through providing incentives for long-range thinking, establishing controls to prevent trade-offs at the expense of strategy, setting realistic short-term goals, and promoting through communication a better understanding of strategic goals.[63]

The most compelling incentive is most likely monetary, although there is ample evidence that managers are influenced by formal recognition and such status enhancements as a larger office and more senior personal secretary. And one should not neglect the impact on managers when they feel that they are engaged in an important, exciting endeavor. The challenge lies in the design of a performance measurement and compensation system that is capable of taking into account, measuring, and rewarding on the basis of specific strategic behavior. The practical problems are so immense that a chief executive is likely to back away from attempting to establish too close and precise a relationship between strategic performance and compensation. For example, how does one define and measure such performance, especially when the results of strategic actions may not be visible for several years? And there is no evaluation system that does not have a high degree of subjectivity, especially as one progresses up the management ladder.[64]

It is probably advisable to avoid attempting to create a complex measurement system and instead to rely on the definition of criteria that, although roughly, do indicate commitment to the strategic plan. A strategic implementation plan, for example, would set forth current-year actions that could be assigned to staff, thus making them measurable. Such strategic actions could be consciously factored into the MBO process, assuring that they are reflected in managers' objectives.

Controls and restraints that prevent managers from trading off "tomorrow for today" require some kind of more or less formal management information system to pinpoint when such trade-offs are occurring or are likely to be made. The simplest and perhaps least costly approach is the use of regular progress review sessions, where senior management review with next-level managers the status of strategic and operational plan implementation. When combined with a reporting system requiring managers to consider explicitly both strategic and operational problems and with a real commitment to in-depth reviews, this informal approach has considerable potential. As Andrews points out, one problem with more formal, quantitative systems, besides their cost to build and operate, is their focus on measurable short-term data, especially from the accounting system.[65]

Putting the right people in the right job is obviously an important element in implementing the strategic plan. A strategy focused on the application of a sophisticated and technologically complex production process would call on different skills and talents than one concentrating on securing a marketing advantage. A fully developed strategy, in setting forth the resource requirements, would specify the numbers and types of persons needed to carry it out. In view of restraints on hiring, firing, and transferring employees in certain situations, an organization is well advised to engage in training and staff development activities.[66] Skills alone, of course, do not determine the "right" person; personality traits may be significant, depending on the demands of the job. It is well known from experience — and supported by some empirical research — that certain personalities have difficulty coping with ambiguous situations or rapid change, while others thrive in such milieus, which they find conducive to innovation and creativity. Generally speaking, it makes sense not to force a person who is most comfortable with order into a turbulent environment, or a very creative person into a highly structured situation.

General Electric surely is at the forefront of large-scale organizations in paying systematic attention to the question of building managerial commitment and support for the implementation of strategies. As a senior GE officer observed, "Proper managerial motivation proved vital to the implementation of our differentiated resource allocation strategy and to the effective strategic control of operations. . . ." Three elements were cited as critical in this process:

☐ In times of economic stress, with pressure to trim back

expenses, the firm's top management not only maintained but also increased financial support for the
twelve "venture opportunities," as well as increasing
funding for research and development.

☐ To the extent feasible, managerial capabilities were
matched with business strategy requirements. For
example, "the more entrepreneurial managers—skilled
in leading change—were matched with our invest/grow
businesses. The most experienced managers were assigned to handle the tough problems of cost control and
investment reduction in weak businesses. . . ."

☐ Bonuses were weighted according to strategic objectives. Different balances between the criteria of current
financial results and future benefit performance were
applied in awarding bonuses. For example, for managers in growth businesses, lower emphasis was placed
on current financial results and higher emphasis on
performance aimed at future benefits.[67]

Implementation Plans

King and Cleland strongly recommend that organizations develop a formal plan for implementing the strategic
planning process—an implementation strategy—that addresses such factors as timing, delegation of operational
matters, and managers' attitudes. As they point out, for
many organizations implementation of strategic planning
may represent "radical" change and should, therefore, be
methodically mapped out. They suggest that the implementation strategy should be a "phased one, a process of
slowly introducing strategic planning in a few organizational elements, and then gradually expanding to the rest
of the organization."[68] They also note that an organization
may not be ready for formal implementation of a process—
that the time may clearly not be right—and that in such
an instance there are a variety of contingency steps that
could move the organization closer to strategic planning,
short of implementing a formal process. These include raising questions relative to the future impact of decisions,
circulating reading material on strategic planning, and
conducting workshops on the subject.[69]

The development of a formal implementation plan can be a valuable part of the implementation of strategies. It is perhaps most usefully treated as the first-year action plan, focusing on the actions required during that year to assure timely achievement of strategic aims. In light of the need for flexibility in strategic planning, it would generally serve no useful purpose to develop detailed implementation plans with a longer scope than the one year. This would be a distinct document from the normal operating plan and budget of the organization, despite being closely related to them. At a minimum, the strategic implementation plan should consist of the following main elements:

☐ Specification of the major actions required during this first implementation year.
☐ Identification of the structural alterations required.
☐ Specification of the resources (financial and nonfinancial) required to carry out the first-year actions, and their sources.

Such a plan would not only assist in monitoring progress in implementing the strategic plan, it would also provide the basis for distributing strategic responsibilities among the managers of the organization.

More on the Human Dimension: Creativity and Innovation

In a number of places thus far, we have cautioned the reader not to underestimate the human role in the process or overestimate the capability of technology and systems. Particular attention has been paid to the heavy contribution that human perception, judgment, intuition, and creativity make to the process of forecasting environmental factors and conditions, assessing their potential implications, and formulating strategies. In light of the widely held belief that increasing environmental turbulence will call for ever more creativity and innovation from organizations as they formulate their strategies, a closer look at these attributes appears justified.

Although there is wide acceptance of the critical role

that creativity plays in strategic planning (Steiner, for example, considers it the most important element in the process), efforts to harness and foster this attribute are hampered by our relatively vague understanding of what it is. Research over the past few years has provided characteristics that appear to distinguish creative persons, such as openness to experience, a sense of humor, independence, highly internalized self-evaluation, preference for complexity, suspicion of authority, the ability to generate ideas rapidly, and originality.[70] In the context of strategic planning, perhaps the most critical expression of creativity is the ability to see both a broader range of strategic options or possibilities and the capability to view familiar objects in different contexts and relationships. From a utilitarian perspective, the value of such brainstorming is that the range of choice is enlarged. Some people's universe of possibilities is significantly larger than others. This is similar to what Vickers calls "instrumental" judgment— "the ability to envisage as possible what has not yet been experienced in fact."[71]

The area of environmental forecasting is an obviously critical testing ground for a person's creative capabilities. The increasing complexity and accelerating rate of change that characterize today's environment call for a wide but sensitive perceptual "filter" capable of picking up faint environmental "signals" and generating alternative environmental scenarios. Ansoff points out that if an organization is "myopic," if its filter is too narrow, its performance expectations "will be inaccurate regardless of the computational refinement of the forecasting methodology."[72]

A recent study of creativity and innovation provides some very useful insights for the organization interested in using creativity properly and fostering it. The author defines innovation as "radical, discontinuous change," and creativity as the "ability to devise and successfully implement such change." He contrasts innovative firms with those that he calls "positional," meaning that they emphasize stability and continuity of operations. Innovative organizations are best adapted to "complex and changing" environmental conditions, while positional organizations are best suited to "simple and stable" environments. His research leads him to believe that a single firm can possess both traits, but only one can predominate at any given time, thus providing management with the difficult challenge of determining which should be in the ascendancy at different points in time.[73]

One would hesitate to offer managers any simple prescriptions for fostering creativity in their organizations. It is possible, however, to offer certain guidelines for chief executives attempting to build more innovative organizations.

☐ Over the long run, schools of management can be encouraged to make creativity and innovation important components of their policy and strategy courses.

☐ Chief executives can pay serious attention to the need to maintain a balance between innovational and operational behavior, varying with changes in the organization's external environment.

☐ In maintaining this balance, chief executives can strive to ensure that:

   a. The requisite number of individuals possessing strong creative abilities is recruited.

   b. The morale and commitment of those creative individuals are maintained through creation of a favorable climate (within reason, of course, since any organization requires a minimum level of discipline).

   c. Formal planning and decision-making processes take into account the need for creativity, thus not inadvertently stifling it.

☐ Chief executives can also make certain that their organizations' staff development and training programs address the elements of creativity and innovation.

☐ Chief executives can encourage tolerance of creative behavior. This sounds deceptively simple; however, in practice, creative individuals can strain the patience of those more accustomed to order in the organization.

Thoughts on Formality in Strategic Planning

The greater part of this introduction has been concerned with the major steps involved in formulating and implementing strategies. With the exception of occasional side comments, the question of the degree of formality in the strategic planning process has not been discussed. Of course, merely by recommending that certain major steps be taken in a particular order, we have acknowledged the need for a minimum level of formality. The strategic planning literature does contain a strong current of reaction against exceedingly formal and structured planning systems; however, it is important that the reader grasp the major criticisms and recommended corrective measures. This brief excursion is not intended to weaken one's faith in the value of formal strategic planning; it is, rather, intended to better prepare the reader to design a realistic and workable planning process in his or her particular organization.

The critics of formalism are by no means anti-planning in their orientation. Their emphasis is on the improvement of the planning process through the correction of flaws that they have identified in the "classical" formal approach. Their reservations and criticisms fall largely into the following three categories, which are closely related and frequently overlap:

☐ The formal strategic planning process is presented as more logical and analytical than it really is or can be. The design is too abstract and fails to take into account the socio-political dynamics at work in any human organization.

☐ The formal strategic planning process is too rigid and slow-moving to respond adequately to a rapidly changing, turbulent environment.

☐ The formal process works against creativity and innovation.

Professor Lorange's recent study of formal planning systems presents a very useful overview of the field. His research indicates that formal long-range planning processes have become a widely accepted and applied management tool, that there appears to be a "reasonably strong empirical verification that formal planning systems have reached a high degree of usefulness and are seen to be generally beneficial." He also reports that there is little evidence verifying the specific benefits of certain planning approaches and that the shortcomings of formal systems have been identified in detail in the literature. He cites one study that suggested the following common pitfalls to avoid in implementing formal systems:

☐ The assumption that the planning function can be delegated to professional planners.

☐ When top management spends too much time on operational matters at the expense of planning.

☐ The failure to formulate goals that provide an adequate framework for strategic planning.

☐ The failure to create a climate conducive to planning.

☐ When top management does not take the time to review plans with those who have developed them.

☐ The lack of an appropriate level of involvement on the part of line managers.

☐ The separation of long-range planning from the normal management process.

☐ The lack of a clear understanding of planning and its potential benefits.

☐ The failure to locate the planning staff high enough in the hierarchy.

☐ The failure to use plans to measure performance.

Lorange notes that the research also indicates that there are several types of planning at work and that a design approach that is "contingency-based" appears to be necessary. This is to say that the critical design features of the particular system should reflect the unique setting of the organization using it.[74]

Perhaps the major fault found with the formal strategic planning process as it is often described is its abstraction, its loss of touch with the realities of human organizational dynamics. These critics believe that the quest for certainty and rationality in turbulent, confusing, and often threatening times leads to an uncritical acceptance of processes that are only superficially rational. As one observer puts it, "Perhaps our lack of wisdom has brought us to a substitution of a ritual of planning for that wisdom. . . ."[75] Another critic observes that the demand for the "appearance of rationality in an area in which knowledge effectively does not exist induces an entrepreneurial pseudo-scientism. . . ."[76]

Perhaps the best known critic of the so-called "rational-comprehensive" model of policy formulation is Charles Lindblom, whose basic objection to the model is that it is not practiced because it does not reflect the real world in which a policy maker works. Lindblom's preferred "branch" method of policy formulation does not involve the clarification of values or objectives prior to consideration of alternative policies, nor does it rely heavily on comprehensive analysis or theory. The branch approach limits analysis "drastically" and substitutes for it a "succession of comparisons"; the basic idea is that the best policy is one that managers reach agreement on, rather than one that meets some abstract notion of appropriateness.[77]

Several other attempts have been made over the years to infuse formal planning with greater realism, and it may be useful to touch briefly on a few. One would focus on the assumptions underlying strategic options during the strategy formulation process. Instead of concentrating on the evaluation of options, the process requires that the assumptions be made explicit and evaluated, after which they are traced back to the options.[78] Another critic has rejected the notion that strategies are solely "intended, a priori guidelines," and has suggested that they are "observed patterns in a decision stream" as well—"evolved, a posteriori consistencies in decisional behavior."[79] A third has proposed an approach that will enable managers to "bind together the contributions of rational systematic analyses, political and power theories, and organizational behavior concepts." The main point is that, as typically described, the formal strategic planning process overemphasizes quantitative factors, which are useful but must be combined with the "vital qualitative, organizational, and power-behavioral factors which so often determine strategic success." This approach utilizes "complicated, largely political, consensus-building processes that are outside the structure of most formal management systems. . . ."[80]

Michael Kami and H. Igor Ansoff are articulate propo-
nents of the view that the rate of environmental change
is increasing so rapidly that a new, more flexible version
of strategic planning must emerge to deal with the faint
"clues" or "signals" that the environment provides. Kami
stresses that the acid test of a planning system's effectiveness is how fast it is able to react, not how well it can
predict. This can be accomplished by focusing the process
on the examination of clues of change rather than "solid"
facts. "A 'clue' is an isolated event which may, however,
have serious consequences if repeated often enough to become a 'fact.' " Unlike in the past, he observes, there is
no time to wait for clues to turn into facts before taking
action, given the rate of change.[81]

Ansoff's "strategic issue management" approach is
intended primarily to serve the organization finding itself
in a highly unstable environment. It is a "real time" system
enabling rapid strategic responses, even in large and complex organizations, through two techniques—scanning the
environment for "weak" signals and acting on them
through ad hoc teams crossing organizational lines.[82] The
basic flaw of many formal strategic planning systems, Ansoff believes, is the requirement for detailed information
before responding, a dangerous characteristic in an unstable environment demanding prompt response. His issue
management approach allows graduated organizational
responses; weak signals are acted upon, but more tenta-
tively than if fuller information were available. Such early
action based on general information should be unfocused
and geared toward enhancing the flexibility of the organization. Ansoff's approach avoids "letting the strategic planning technology determine the information needs" of an
organization and instead enables the organization to
"determine what planning and action are *feasible* as
strategic information becomes available in the course of
the threat/opportunity."[83]

The foregoing discussion of creativity and innovation
pointed out the value of a high degree of freedom, openness, and flexibility to the exercise of both functions. There
is no question that overformalizing every step of the plan-

ning process can hamper the exercise of creativity. An experienced strategic management consultant observed in a recent article that "the more quantitatively oriented and sophisticated a planning process becomes, the harder it is for most managers to come up with fresh approaches. By its very nature, the system tends to suppress new ideas that may only be questions, vague feelings, or hunches at the start."[84]

The "bottom line" of our discussion of formalism in planning is not in any way a rejection of the value or practicality of strategic planning. It is, rather, a strong injunction not to view strategic planning as a process that is neater, more precise, and more amenable to scientific technique than is possible in the real world. A balanced approach is clearly in order in undertaking the design and implementation of strategic planning. A formal, rational process, drawing on quantitative analysis, must be balanced by an appreciation for the human factors and should not be pursued at the expense of timeliness, creativity, and political realism.[85]

As King and Cleland point out, it is important that the formal planning process be evaluated regularly to ensure that it is effective. As they note, a bad planning system may be worse than no formal process. Short of the ultimate test of a planning process—the impact of the decisions and plans generated—there are a variety of measurement standards that could be applied, including:

- [ ] Management participation in planning.
- [ ] The structure for planning.
- [ ] The data bases created and utilized.
- [ ] The climate for planning in the organization.
- [ ] The steps followed—such as the environmental scan, the identification of strategic options, and the selection of strategies.[86]

Planning Support—
the Planning Office and Director

Most, if not all, large organizations have central planning offices with responsibility for supporting their long-range planning efforts. Staffing obviously varies with the size and complexity of the particular organization, as well as the nature of the planning process. In multidivisional organizations, it is common to find divisional planning units that work with, if they do not report to, the central planning office.

Generally speaking, such central planning offices are responsible for: design, coordination, and facilitation of the planning process; technical assistance to line units; review of plans; and special studies and analyses for senior management. There is resolute consensus in the literature that the central planning office should never *do* the planning for the corporation; rather, it should assist line managers to do it themselves. There is also general agreement that the central planning office should be directly responsible to the chief executive, or at least to a very high ranking officer of the organization.

Steiner has suggested that the central planning office perform the following seven functions:

- ☐ Assist top management in the formulation of the firm's long-range objectives, strategies, and policies.
- ☐ Coordinate and integrate the planning that is done at different levels of the organization, including, when appropriate, consolidation of plans into one planning document.
- ☐ Provide guidance to the operating divisions in their planning, including such procedural guidance as planning manuals and such substantive guidance as planning assumptions, environmental forecasts, and special studies.
- ☐ Review and evaluate plans for top management.
- ☐ Assist managers who lack planning expertise in preparing their plans.
- ☐ Conduct special studies and analyses for top management.
- ☐ Provide assistance to top management in strategy formulation in lieu of available assistance in the operating divisions.[87]

Conference Board research indicates that the effectiveness of the planning office depends most heavily on four factors:

- ☐ The existence of a close, positive relationship between the planning director and the chief executive.
- ☐ Whether the office's charter mandates it to play a creative, substantive role or a largely administrative, bureaucratic role.
- ☐ The capability of the planning staff.
- ☐ Acceptance of the office by line managers.

The last factor is achievable only through serious effort on the part of the planning director and staff. Even with the strong support of the chief executive, the planning staff must be very sensitive to nuances in the internal socio-political environment, must build positive relationships based on mutual respect with line managers, and must generally be self-effacing. Though difficult, it is essential that the office be at the same time strong and influential on the one hand and unthreatening to line management on the other.[88]

Appointment of the planning director may be the most important decision the chief executive makes with regard to building an effective planning process. The planning director should, of course, possess those characteristics associated with all senior executives, including maturity, poise, intelligence and creativity, willingness to take risks, and strong interpersonal skills such as tact and persuasiveness. A primary determinant of the director's success is his or her relationship with the chief executive, which must be characterized by mutual trust, respect, and understanding.

Steiner suggests that the planning director must "above all" understand that his or her role is not to make decisions. The director must "sell" rather than "tell" his views and, regardless of the situation, he must avoid— "indeed he must lean backward to avoid giving an impression that he makes decisions for line action."[89]

Summary

This introduction to the theory and practice of strategic planning has provided an overview of the historical development of long-range planning, has defined the key terms, described in some detail the basic steps in strategic planning, and has addressed certain special issues: creativity and innovation, the formality of planning processes, and the role and functions of the planning office. The primary objective has been to present a fairly accurate and complete picture of this complex and fast-changing field within a very brief compass. While not wanting to introduce more detail than would truly be useful in understanding the main concepts and techniques, every effort has been made to avoid meaningless generalizations and glib little golden rules. Finally, it should be noted that there is currently underway at the Columbia University Graduate School of Business a major research project that is intended to evaluate rigorously the ultimate contribution of strategic planning to a variety of business organizations. As the findings and conclusions become available over the next several years, it is reasonable to expect that more comprehension and discipline will characterize the application of strategic planning.

Although it is clear that no single, universal model for strategic planning dominates, a general framework does emerge, and its realism—and hence its relevance—is rooted in its diversity, its reflection of a wide variety of techniques and perspectives. This framework consists of the following major elements:

☐ The need for any organization to formulate strategies aimed at an optimal adaptation to the present and future environment, making the best feasible use of the organization's existing and potential resources in capitalizing on environmental opportunities and limiting the impact of negative forces.

☐ The efficacy of following certain broad steps in formulating strategies:

  a. Determining an organization's strategic profile.

  b. Identifying, forecasting, and assessing the impact of external environmental factors and conditions relevant to the organization, including opportunities and constraints.

    c. Assessing internal resources, strengths, and weaknesses.

    d. After a relatively freewheeling process of identifying strategic possibilities, arriving at an overall strategy for the organization most in harmony with its capabilities and environmental conditions, and then developing specific strategies, including the specification of resource requirements.

☐ The importance of devoting serious attention to implementation, including the conscious design for: the role of the chief executive, organizational structure, linking strategy to operations, securing managerial support and commitment, and developing a formal and communicated implementation plan.

☐ The need to guard against rigidity and overformality of systems and processes, both of which can force an organization out of tune with its environment. This is especially critical in times of environmental turbulence when it will be advisable to bypass steps in the formal planning process in order to promote timely organizational responses.

☐ The recognition that the strategic planning process is far more than a matter of technology and analytical technique and the acceptance and creative management of the socio-political dimension of planning, with its elements of negotiation and incremental decision making.

☐ The recognition of the importance of human perceptiveness and creativity in strategic planning, and the need to pay conscious attention to fostering these qualities.

☐ The requirement that strategic planning processes be tailored to particular organizations, with their unique characteristics, history and traditions, and decision-making culture.

In conclusion, it is suggested that strategic planning represents a powerful resource for the more effective management of organizations, but only if it is very carefully applied with a full understanding of its limitations as well as its strengths. In a large, complex organization, the strategic planning process can be both time consuming and painful; there is no easy way to put into practice such sophisticated techniques as those called for in strategic planning. As has already been noted, it has become all too common for an organization to design an elaborate long-range planning process that yields very little strategic benefit because it is focused on the documentation of current activities and includes only a perfunctory scan of the environment. Not only is valuable time wasted, but the organization is likely to foster the dangerous illusion of being in command of its own destiny. Let no chief executive be unaware that if strategic planning is to yield benefits in his or her organization, it will claim time and energy in abundance, as well as perhaps requiring a large financial investment. There is ample evidence that the alternative, however, is today unacceptably risky.

CHAPTER I NOTES

1. Peter Lorange, "Formal Planning Systems: Their Role in Strategy Formulation and Implementation," in *Strategic Management: A New View of Business Policy and Planning*, ed. Dan E. Schendel and Charles W. Hofer (Boston: Little, Brown and Company, 1979), p. 228.

2. Derek F. Channon, "Commentary," in Schendel and Hofer, pp. 123–125.

3. H. Igor Ansoff, *Strategic Management* (New York: John Wiley and Sons, 1979), pp. 22–23. See also, Ansoff, "The Changing Shape of the Strategic Problem," in Schendel and Hofer, pp. 31–32.

4. Ansoff, *Strategic Management*, pp. 23–24. See also, Ansoff, "Changing Shape," in Schendel and Hofer, pp. 32–33.

5. Ansoff, "Changing Shape," p. 35. See also, Ansoff, *Strategic Management*, pp. 25–29.

6. Russell L. Ackoff, *A Concept of Corporate Planning* (New York: John Wiley and Sons, Inc., 1970), p. 4.

7. Alfred D. Chandler, Jr., *Strategy and Structure: Chapters in the History of the Industrial Enterprise* (Cambridge: The M.I.T. Press, 1962), p. 13.

8. George A. Steiner, *Top Management Planning* (London: The Macmillan Company, 1969), p. 238.

9. Richard F. Vancil, "Strategy Formulation in Complex Organizations," *Sloan Management Review* 17 (Winter 1976): 1–2.

10. William R. King and David I. Cleland, *Strategic Planning and Policy* (New York: Van Nostrand Reinhold, 1978), p. 15.

11. George A. Steiner and John B. Miner, *Management Policy and Strategy: Text, Readings, and Cases* (New York: Macmillan Publishing Co., 1977), p. 21. See also, Steiner, *Top Management Planning*, pp. 239–240.

12. Schendel and Hofer, *Strategic Management*, p. 11.

13. Steiner and Miner, *Management Policy*, p. 7.

14. Hugo E. R. Uyterhoeven, Robert W. Ackerman, and John W. Rosenblum, *Strategy and Organization: Text and Cases in General Management* (Homewood: Richard D. Irwin, Inc., 1973), pp. 34–35.

15. Steiner and Miner, *Management Policy*, p. 41.

16. Carnegie Foundation for the Advancement of Teaching, *More Than Survival: Prospects for Higher Education in a Period of Uncertainty* (San Francisco: Jossey-Bass Publishers, 1975), p. 49.

17. James M. Utterback, "Environmental Analysis and Forecasting," in Schendel and Hofer, p. 135.

18. King and Cleland, *Strategic Planning*, pp. 221–242.

19. Utterback, "Environmental Analysis," pp. 136–138.

20. Ibid., pp. 136–137. See also, John C. Chambers and Satinder K. Mullick, "Forecasting for Planning," in *Corporate Planning: Techniques and Applications*, ed. Robert J. Allio and Malcolm W. Pennington (New York: AMACOM, 1979), pp. 324–325.

21. Utterback, "Environmental Analysis," pp. 137–138.

22. Ibid., 137. See also, Thomas H. Naylor, *Corporate Planning Models* (Manila, Philippines: Addison-Wesley Publishing Company, Inc., 1979), p. 1.

23. The Conference Board, *Planning Under Uncertainty: Multiple Scenarios and Contingency Planning* (New York: The Conference Board, Inc., 1978), pp. 1–10.

24. Chambers and Mullick, "Forecasting," pp. 325–326.

25. Standley Hoch, "Strategic Management in GE" (address delivered at Annual Meeting of the Council of State Planning Agencies, New Orleans, September 26, 1980), p. 8.

26. Michael G. Allen, "Diagramming GE's Planning for What's Watt," in Allio and Pennington, pp. 213–214.

27. American Telephone and Telegraph Company, *The Bell System Emerging Issues Program* (1980), pp. 1–7.

28. Ansoff, *Strategic Management*, pp. 76–89.

29. Uyterhoeven, Ackerman, and Rosenblum, *Strategy and Organization*, pp. 40–47.

30. Ibid., p. 48.

31. Richard F. Vancil and Peter Lorange, "Strategic Planning in Diversified Companies," *Harvard Business Review* 53 (January–February 1975): 81–83.

32. John H. Grant and William R. King, "Strategy Formulation: Analytical and Normative Models," in Schendel and Hofer, pp. 111–113.

33. Channon, "Commentary," pp. 123–126.

34. Ibid., p. 126.

35. Yoram Wind and Vijay Mahajan, "Designing Product and Business Portfolios," *Harvard Business Review* 59 (January–February 1981): 155–157.

36. Channon, "Commentary," p. 126. Allio and Pennington, *Corporate Planning*, Introduction, pp. 17–18. Wind and Mahajan, "Designing Portfolios," p. 158.

37. Grant and King, "Strategy Formulation," p. 117. Allio and Pennington, *Corporate Planning*, p. 18.

38. Channon, "Commentary," p. 128. Wind and Mahajan, "Designing Portfolios," p. 158.

39. Channon, "Commentary," pp. 128–129. Allio and Pennington, *Corporate Planning*, pp. 18–19.

40. Wind and Mahajan, "Designing Portfolios," pp. 158–165.

41. Uyterhoeven, Ackerman, and Rosenblum, *Strategy and Organization*, pp. 59–62.

42. Schendel and Hofer, *Strategic Management*, pp. 190–193.

43. Steiner and Miner, *Management Policy*, pp. 219–221. See also, King and Cleland, *Strategic Planning*, pp. 354–356.

44. Steiner, *Top Management Planning*, p. 88.

45. Ansoff, *Strategic Management*, pp. 129–130.

46. Ibid., p. 139.

47. Kenneth Andrews, *The Concept of Corporate Strategy* (Homewood: Dow Jones-Irwin, Inc., 1971), pp. 227–228.

48. The Conference Board, *Planning and the Chief Executive* (New York: The Conference Board, Inc., 1972), pp. 19–20.

49. Steiner, *Planning*, pp. 92–93.

50. King and Cleland, *Strategic Planning*, pp. 294–295.

51. Chandler, *Strategy and Structure*, pp. 13–16.

52. Jay R. Galbraith and Daniel A. Nathanson, "The Role of Organizational Structure and Process in Strategy Implementation," in Schendel and Hofer, pp. 262–269. See also, Galbraith and Nathanson, *Strategy Implementation: The Role of Structure and Process* (St. Paul: West Publishing Co., 1979), pp. 139–140.

53. Andrews, *Corporate Strategy*, pp. 188–190.

54. Steiner, *Planning*, pp. 229–301.

55. John H. Hobbs and Donald F. Heany, "Coupling Strategy to Operating Plans," *Harvard Business Review* 55 (May–June 1977): 123–126.

56. J. K. Shank, E. G. Niblock, and W. T. Sandalls, "Balance 'Creativity' and 'Practicality' in Formal Planning," *Harvard Business Review* 51 (January–February 1973): 87–92.

57. Steiner and Miner, *Management Policy*, pp. 627–639.

58. Warren C. Bennis, *Changing Organizations: Essays on the Development and Evolution of Human Organization* (New York: McGraw-Hill Book Company, 1966), p. 176.

59. Sir Geoffrey Vickers, *The Art of Judgment: A Study of Policy Making* (New York: Basic Books, Inc., 1965), p. 93.

60. Steiner and Miner, *Management Policy*, pp. 642–643.

61. Andrews, *Corporate Strategy*, p. 205.

62. Ibid., p. 200.

63. Robert L. Banks and Steven C. Wheelwright, "Operations vs. Strategy: Trading Tomorrow for Today," *Harvard Business Review* 57 (May–June 1979): 116–119.

64. Analog Devices has apparently successfully tested a bonus system recognizing contributions to strategic objectives, but this appears to be a very rare phenomenon. See, Ray Stata and Modesto A. Maidique, "Bonus System for Balanced Strategy," *Harvard Business Review* 58 (November–December 1980): 156–163.

65. Andrews, *Corporate Strategy*, pp. 212–214.

66. Ibid., p. 219.

67. Allen, "Diagramming GE's Planning," pp. 217–218.

68. King and Cleland, *Strategic Planning*, p. 327.

69. Ibid., pp. 343–345.

70. Steiner, *Planning*, pp. 352–356. See also, Harry Nystrom, *Creativity and Innovation* (Toronto: John Wiley and Sons, 1979), p. 57.

71. Vickers, *Judgment*, p. 87.

72. Ansoff, *Strategic Management*, pp. 145–147.

73. Nystrom, *Creativity*, pp. 1–6.

74. Lorange, "Formal Planning Systems," pp. 226–235.

75. Emerson C. Shuck, "The New Planning and an Old Pragmatism," *The Journal of Higher Education* 48 (September–October 1977): 601.

76. Stephen P. Dresh, "A Critique of Planning Models for Postsecondary Education," *The Journal of Higher Education* 46 (May–June 1975): 247–248.

77. Charles E. Lindblom, "The Science of Muddling Through," in *Business Strategy*, ed. H. Igor Ansoff (New York: Penguin Books, 1969), pp. 44–55.

78. James R. Emshoff and Arthur Finnel, "Defining Corporate Strategy: A Case Study Using Strategic Assumptions Analysis," *Sloan Management Review* 20 (Spring 1979): 41–42.

79. Henry Mintzberg, "Patterns in Strategy Formation," *Management Science* 24 (May 1978): 935. See also, Henry Mintzberg, "Strategy Making in Three Modes," *California Management Review* 16 (Winter 1973): 45–48.

80. James Brian Quinn, "Strategic Change: 'Logical Incrementalism,'" *Sloan Management Review* 20 (Fall 1978): 7–19. See also, James Brian Quinn, "Strategic Goals: Process and Politics," *Sloan Management Review* 19 (Fall 1977): 21–29; 36.

81. Michael J. Kami, "Planning and Planners in the Age of Discontinuity" (address delivered at the Planning Conference, "Planning for the Fourth Quarter Century," San Francisco, May 21–24, 1975).

82. H. Igor Ansoff, "The State of Practice in Planning Systems," *Sloan Management Review* 18 (Winter 1977): 22.

83. H. Igor Ansoff, "Managing Strategic Surprise by Response to Weak Signals," *California Management Review* 18 (Winter 1975): 21–23.

84. J. Quincy Hunsicker, "The Malaise of Strategic Planning," *Management Review* 64 (March 1980): 8.

85. Harold W. Fox, "The Frontiers of Strategic Planning: Intuition or Formal Models," *Management Review* 70 (April 1981): 8–9.

86. King and Cleland, *Strategic Planning*, pp. 350–355.

87. Steiner, *Planning*, pp. 116–121.

88. The Conference Board, *Planning and the Chief Executive*, pp. 33–34.

89. Steiner, *Planning*, pp. 128–129. See also, King and Cleland, *Strategic Planning*, p. 342.

CHAPTER II

The Nexus: Relating Successful Business Experience to Contemporary Management Requirements in Government

Introduction

▥▶ This chapter presents an overview of the development and status of planning in state government. Without attempting a comprehensive survey of current planning activities, some attention is given notable examples that illustrate the variety of approaches being used. The purpose of this overview is to determine what kind of foundation has been laid for the possible application of strategic planning in state government. Also, consideration is accorded those features of the public sector that are commonly considered to distinguish it from the for-profit sector and that might, therefore, wisely be taken into account in designing and implementing strategic planning processes in state government. The aim is to equip governors and their senior executives with an understanding of the complexities and barriers that will be encountered in realizing the substantial potential benefits of strategic planning in state government.

Although there are surely differences between the two sectors that merit mention, and that should be consciously considered in formulating a planning program, they have yet to be thoroughly examined and their practical implications documented. Furthermore, the distinctions appear to be blurring, and the similarities between the governmental and for-profit sectors are becoming ever more apparent. Both sectors perform the major functions involved in the leadership and management of large-scale organizations, even if there are significant differences in the purposes and end results of their activities. Thus, the foremost question today is how to manage large organizations—public and for-profit—effectively in a time of increasing environmental turbulence.

This section basically reflects a commitment to be realistic in providing guidance to state managers in utilizing strategic planning techniques. Being realistic, of course, means having a clear picture of the difficulties and pitfalls that might be encountered in pursuing a course of action. On the one hand, it is hardly appealing to arm those who are philosophically opposed to planning with further reasons why "it" cannot be done. On the other, there is every reason to avoid the common trap of so extolling the virtues of planning and so minimizing the constraints that the unrealism of the advice being proffered is all too obvious. While some detractors may relish building such "straw men" and proceeding to demolish them under the guise of criticism, serious planning advocates have likewise been known to build their own straw men through their unrestrained enthusiasm and missionary zeal. Such lack of restraint has been cited as an element in the relatively quick and complete demise of the planning, programming, budgeting system (PPBS) in the Federal government.

It would be difficult to imagine a time more auspicious for the implementation of strategic planning techniques in state government. As the preceding chapter pointed out, a substantial body of theory has developed over the past twenty years or so, and the fund of practical experience in the for-profit sector is rapidly growing. Thus there are models and lessons to guide state managers. Granted, use of these developing aids will require detailed attention to the translation of for-profit knowledge into a language that is meaningful in the public context.

The need and the opportunity also make this an auspicious time for applying strategic planning in the governance and management of state government. It is abundantly clear that current management systems and practices equip state governments to cope effectively neither with the rapid growth that a small number are experiencing nor with the much more widespread contraction of economies and populations.[1] The many hard choices that must be made at one time can no longer be handled effectively by current management systems, and the need for new approaches is obvious and urgent. On the most positive side, it appears that the nation is entering a period during which states will have the opportunity to play a considerably larger role in the management of our Federal system. Public opinion has long favored the reduction of the size and influence of the government, and the current administration in Washington appears committed to reducing Federal control of state and local affairs.

The contraction of the Federal government's role can be a positive challenge—an opportunity—to the states to embrace a more influential role in the Federal system of governance. Or it can be viewed as only a hardship to be endured until Federal largess begins to flow once again. It is believed that the well-planned, carefully paced application of strategic planning by state governments can contribute substantially to equipping states to play the more positive and creative role.

State Planning: An Overview

This is not the appropriate place to trace the development of state planning in detail; such has been done in the Council of State Planning Agencies' State Planning Series. However, a review of the broad aspects of this development and a summary of the current status of planning in state government, drawing on important illustrative examples, will provide the context for an examination of the possible applications of strategic planning.

State governments are not known for taking a leadership role in planning innovation, and the subject of state planning has not attracted, relatively speaking, notable academic attention; but it should be observed at the start of this discussion that considerable planning, covering a wide variety of types and techniques, is currently being done in state government. And the field of state planning is hardly static; as states have assumed wider governance responsibilities, new approaches to planning have been formulated and tested. Two caveats do seem in order in assessing the progress made in planning at the state level. First, the history of state planning is relatively brief and somewhat truncated. Second, the tremendous variation among the states in the quantity, scope, and depth of planning makes generalizing about the firmness of the state planning foundation impossible. Each state must be examined individually in terms of its planning, and perhaps the only general counsel that can be safely offered is to err on the side of conservatism and to avoid overestimating the strength of the planning foundation in formulating a strategic planning program.

Much of the brief history of state planning is a story of response and reaction to Federal government initiatives, beginning in the 1930s with the establishment of state planning boards and commissions in response to the Federal Public Works Administration's National Resources Planning Board. Such early efforts were oriented toward comprehensive physical plans. This initial major developmental phase was largely ended by World War II, which naturally commanded the nation's attention. A period of very rapid growth in state planning began in the 1950s, once again largely in response to Federal legislation mandating planning by the states and, as before, focused on comprehensive physical and natural resource planning. It has been observed that "most Governors and state legislatures prior to 1968 saw the planning roles of state government concerned primarily with capital facilities location . . . and industrial development."[2]

If Federal planning requirements were a blessing, that blessing was frequently well disguised. Far from taking an orderly, integrated approach to planning, the Federal government was content to impose a myriad of separate planning requirements through different funding programs, resulting in inevitable confusion and frustration. For example, during 1955–56, Georgia was preparing eighty separate program plans as a condition for the receipt of Federal dollars.[3]

The 1960s saw states beginning to put their own planning houses in order so as not to continue to play the puppet, dancing madly on Federal strings. The decade also saw significant Federal efforts to bring order into the planning environment, most particularly through Office of Management and Budget Circular A-95, which required the review of Federal grant applications at areawide and state levels for compliance with areawide and state planning. States began to provide stronger planning direction and coordination during the decade, and evident planning advances included the preparation of statewide development plans in New York and California.[4]

The state planning function developed rapidly in scope, organization, and focus during the late 1960s and the 1970s. Although economic and physical planning continued to predominate, state planning was extended to a variety of areas, such as health, human services, regional and local planning, environmental protection, and local government assistance. During this period, twenty states underwent comprehensive administrative reorganization, and another twenty partial reorganization. One of the significant results was the location of an increasing number of state planning agencies in or close to the Governor's office. By 1977, thirty-one states had located the planning agency within the Governor's office or the executive department, and eight states within a department of administration along with budget and other management support functions. To one observer, this can be taken to mean that planning had become "an integral part of policy development in a government organization more capable of being managed."[5]

A 1967 survey indicated that "many state legislatures perceived the state planning agency's central role to be assisting in the decision-making process at the state level, primarily by advising and otherwise assisting the governor and others in the state executive branch." The hierarchy of activities performed by state planning agencies that emerged from the study were: (1) provision of advice to the

Governor; (2) review and coordination of planning; (3) actual preparation of the plans; and (4) work with the legislature. As the authors point out, "There is nothing in these data to alter our sense of the increasing chief-executive orientation of the state planning function."[6]

A 1977 study of the legal foundation for state planning published by the Council of State Planning Agencies indicated that a wide range of planning responsibilities was required of state planning agencies by legislation. Thirty-four states, for example, had enacted legislation requiring the development of a four- to six-year comprehensive or master plan (even though the author's interviews indicated that such plans were "seldom produced and almost never used"). Twenty-three states required the planning agency to do specific functional planning, thirty-two required the agency to develop policy statements, forty-two to perform policy research, and fifty to coordinate the planning of other state agencies. Thirty-one states had designated the planning agency as their A-95 clearinghouse and as the administrator of the Economic Development Administration's economic resource planning process.[7]

The evaluation of the effectiveness of state planning is beyond the scope of this book; a meaningful assessment would require state-by-state research, combining reviews of planning products and system designs with actual on-site investigations into the use and implementation of plans. In general, however, there is no question that much planning is occurring, although the extent to which it is being used is difficult to determine. A 1977 survey of the American Institute of Planners, for example, found that "the majority of States operate their growth policies through formal executive branch preparation of a state policy plan or set of plans and review of the programs and functional plans of line agencies in light of the established policy."[8] A study of state policy instruments done the same year, however, provides some basis for reserving judgment as to the effectiveness of state planning. Although more than 70 percent of the respondents indicated that they used planning as a policy instrument often or sometimes, approximately 50 percent felt that it was "ineffective, neutral or nonassessable." The authors suggested that the fact that so much state planning was being done in response to Federal requirements may account for this ambiguous, if not negative, result.[9]

A 1980 study of urban strategy development in ten states, conducted by the National Academy of Public Administration for the U.S. Department of Housing and Urban Development, found that nine of the ten had formulated strategies that roughly conform to the definition used in this book (including goals, programs, and implementation processes) since 1977. Despite a wide variation in the stages of development and kinds of documentation, it is significant that all but one of this large (approximately 40 percent of the U.S. population) and diverse (geographically and in terms of problems faced—economic decline and population loss on the one hand, growth on the other) sample were engaged in serious efforts to formulate more comprehensive and long-range approaches to urban development. The author of the study concludes that the state planning efforts being reported "would seem to justify" the belief of those formulating strategies that "judicious application of state powers in the regulatory area, in land use and environmental protection and through the timing and staging of public investments can shape and influence private market decisions and yield positive, long-term results."[10]

One indicator of the effectiveness of state planning is the effectiveness of the state planning agency. As another study published by the Council of State Planning Agencies has pointed out, planning agencies that provide effective support to the Governor "depend upon a personal relationship between planning personnel and the chief executive, require very rapid response capability, and involve only infrequently the heavy documentation and elaborate analyses that planners are prone to submit." The checklist that this author provides for determining whether the planning agency is supplying effective assistance to the Governor includes such items as planning staff participation in the Governor's office staff meetings, the Governor's expectation that the planning director will initiate new policies, and the Governor's use of the agency for information, analysis, and recommendations in crisis situations.[11]

Interviews with persons knowledgeable about planning in their states and a highly selective review of state planning documentation, although not constituting a scientific sampling on which to base generalizations, proved very helpful in gaining a better understanding of the status of state planning—of its diversity, extent, and scope. The following points provide a framework for the review of documentation that follows:

☐ Stated intentions, whether conveyed in gubernatorial messages or embodied in formal planning process descriptions, can be misleading if taken at face value. Subsequent actions and events give such aims and aspirations their meaning. There is reason to believe, for example, that despite the articulation of rather ambitious planning objectives in certain states, the current fiscal crisis has focused attention almost exclusively on day-to-day budget balancing despite the fact that such short-sighted budget cutting may lead to even more serious fiscal problems in the future. The examples of plans and "plans to plan" that we will discuss are intended to illustrate the variety of planning activity presently occurring at the state level. An in-depth study of one or more cases would be useful not only to evaluate the effectiveness of a given planning approach, but also to understand better the dynamics at work in state planning.

☐ Although there is apparently no case of a formal, comprehensive strategic planning system being designed and implemented in a state government, the examples that follow illustrate that serious attempts to transcend, to provide a more rational framework for, the traditional policy formulation and incremental budgeting processes have at least been conceptualized, if not in every case carried through completely. In one large state, not discussed below, the planning office is presently attempting to apply certain of the more powerful analytical techniques of strategic planning, including most notably a test of portfolio matrices.

☐ The illustrations range over a wide spectrum from the more strategic in reach to the more operational. California provides an example of a comprehensive, integrated plan with several strategic characteristics in a single programmatic area—natural resources, and Colorado offers an excellent example of public-private sector collaboration in the process of identifying, forecasting, and assessing the implications of national and state environmental conditions. Utah, Minnesota, Alaska, and Pennsylvania illustrate very important attempts to interject policy guidance into the operational and capital resource allocation processes.

☐ To repeat an important caveat: taken alone, the documentation reviewed below can obviously be misleading. No matter how impressive the conceptual design, technical approach, or the detailed process, the only real test of effectiveness is whether the planning process generates a plan that is ultimately implemented in a useful, thorough, and timely fashion.

"Investing for Prosperity," a product of the Resources Agency of the State of California, is in several respects an impressive strategic document. It "outlines goals of resource investments between now and the year 2000. It charts a destiny course for the Resources Agency describing positive, realistic actions that will halt resource decline and provide greater hope for future Californians." This twenty-year plan consists of three main elements:

☐ A brief issue analysis of each of the resources being addressed (e.g., fish and wildlife, water, soils).

☐ A set of largely measurable goals for each resource over the twenty-year period, e.g., "Reduce imports of forest products into California from 4.8 to 1.8 billion board feet."

☐ A two-year implementation plan for each resource, setting forth specific goals closely tied to the twenty-year goals, e.g., "Complete 81 urban forestry projects which will plant 112,500 trees throughout the urban areas of the State and involve the active participation of local citizens."

"Investing for Prosperity" makes a critical connection with the resource allocation process that is probably quite rare in public sector planning. The plan concludes with a section of several pages identifying many of the elements contained in the two-year implementation plans being proposed in the Governor's Budget for funding in 1981–82. Perhaps as important as the document's technical completeness is that it is clearly aimed at a wider audience than professional planners or state government bureaucrats. It is obviously well crafted: the prose is clear, and the format promotes a logical, natural flow of ideas, taking the reader on a relatively painless, perhaps even pleasant, journey. Unlike many long-range plans, "Investing for Prosperity" is of readable length, just over fifty pages. The reader cannot help but be impressed by the attempt to provide a philosophical framework for the goals being recommended in the plan. One of the prefatory pages, headed "Recognition of the Public Trust," conveys the central message that a civilization wastes its natural resources at great peril to its survival by quoting Livy, Theodore Roosevelt, the Paley Commission Report to President Truman, and Governor Brown. The introduction provides essential background to the reader by briefly describing several legislative enactments related to the goals of the plan, and the section entitled "Public Trust" states four "guiding principles" that constitute the philosophy undergirding the twenty- and two-year goals.

A document produced by the Blue Ribbon Panel of the state of Colorado, "Private Choices, Public Strategies," does an admirable job of environmental analyses and forecasting, setting forth planning assumptions and assessing the resources available and required to carry out the investment strategies being recommended. A noteworthy element of this twenty-year plan for using public and private investment to cope with anticipated growth is the apparently active involvement of for-profit-sector leadership in producing the document and the conscious consideration of private, as well as public, investment requirements.

"Private Choices, Public Strategies" presents, after a summary chapter, relatively detailed forecasts of the national and state economies and demographic conditions for the 1980–85 and 1985–2000 periods. Assumptions relative to the general economy, labor force, population, energy, and other factors are followed by "outlooks" for the two periods. The following excerpt is illustrative of the approach to forecasting; it relates to the 1985–2000 outlook for Colorado:

> The trade (wholesale and retail) and services (including finance) sectors will increase their domination of the state's economy, employing 55% of the state's work force by the year 2000. This growth is a reflection of the movement of the U.S. economy into post-industrial development, the importance of Denver to the Rocky Mountain West, and the growth in business services to support the energy and electronics industries.

The environmental forecasts are supported by extensive charts, tables, and figures in a separate volume of appendixes.

A chapter setting forth current state service level revenue and expenditure forecasts to the year 2000, with a detailed explanation of the methodology used, its limitations, and a thorough orientation on state financing, is followed by a final section identifying public and private capital investment needs and financing approaches, including options to be explored, e.g., "creation of a broad growth and development authority to make grants, underwrite or guarantee loans, or to raise revenue through bond sales."

The Colorado document represents a superb beginning for strategic planning; after the searching look at the national and state environments, the forecast of revenues and expenditures of state government, and the identification of capital investment needs, along with a brief review of financing options, there is no attempt to develop action plans or strategies for alternative courses of action. The California and Colorado documents would, if combined, come very close to being a complete strategic plan.

A March 1980 memorandum to Utah department heads and planners, stating that a "central theme" of the

Governor's administration is "the need to manage the state's future growth through long range planning" sets forth a systematic process for achieving such growth management, consisting of four major elements: (1) the "Growth Management Strategy"; (2) the state capital budget; (3) the "Community Investment Strategy"; and (4) the "Agenda for the Eighties Conference." Focusing on the physical development needs of Utah, the process ties capital budgeting to an overall policy framework and more detailed strategies. The first step is the articulation by the Governor of a "preliminary policy statement" setting forth briefly the "problem areas, background, issues, major principles . . . and proposed actions." The more detailed growth management strategy "indicates specific actions and programs to implement" the broad policy. Developed by the state agencies, the strategy is during the first year to consist basically of a "physical needs assessment." Presumably, the ten-year capital facilities plan and five-year capital budget program are developed within the framework of the growth policy.

Utah's "Community Investment Strategy" is intended, within a framework of the growth policy and capital budget, to "coordinate and prioritize state and federal funds to local government for capital improvements." A priority list of local capital improvement projects is to be developed, and the Governor is to use his political influence to ensure that higher priority projects are given first consideration by the state legislature and Congress. The "Agenda for the Eighties Conference" appears to be aimed at securing the participation of civic leadership in the identification of issues and formulation of policy options, as well as assessing the state's planning process plans. Incidental to this planning reform, Utah is developing an integrated annual planning and budgeting cycle.

The Minnesota planning approach, as described in a June 1980 document, "Overview of a Governor's General Management Process," is a prime example of the explicit attention given to the responsibility of the Governor to stamp the process with his philosophy and management style. For example, a draft memorandum, "The Emerging

Personality of the Quie Administration," circulated by the Governor, sets forth a list of characteristics that suggest "the kind of administration Governor Quie would like to see develop—a 'personality' that will be expressed through specific goals and activities" formulated by line agencies. Five characteristics describe the "vision" of the administration; for example, it "seeks new partnerships and alliances with the non-governmental sector for the public good." Among the six characteristics of its "style" is the belief that "lasting progress is achieved more through reconciliation of differences than overbearing advocacy." Its "view of government" requests people "to keep a sane estimate of government's ability to solve human problems."

The focus of the Minnesota process is on ensuring that the budget planning process reflects the priority issues and sub-issues articulated by the Governor, after extensive participation from line agencies, rather than on the formulation of long-run strategies for the state. It is likely that this approach—formulating policies and goals focused on budget preparation—is much more commonly practiced in state government than longer-range planning focusing on a reexamination of the purpose and goals of state government in the context of the future five or ten or more years. Major fiscal problems, however, have recently shifted attention away from the planning process.

In Alaska, for example, the Governor's priorities are expressed as "policy themes" in the budgeting instructions as part of a process that is "structured in such a way as to provide incentives for agencies to develop annual requests that conform to the policy themes." And Pennsylvania's "Program Policy Guidelines for Preparation of the 1980–81 Executive Budget," observing that the Governor's annual budget proposal is "the single most important policy and planning document of the Administration," provides the agencies with a set of general objectives in six program areas (e.g., energy, transportation) to guide detailed budget preparation.

The Budget Connection

Budgeting, not long-range planning, has long been,

and still is, the preeminent management tool and executive decision-making process in the public sector, including state government. As was pointed out in the preceding chapter, many view the budget as strategic planning's anchor in reality, although there are distinct dangers involved in tying long-range planning and budgeting too closely. Budgeting has been the principal vehicle for management innovation in state government, and at the same time perhaps the greatest barrier to innovation. As the final fifth of this century begins, it is probably safe to say that the tried and true, oft-maligned object-of-expenditure budget continues to serve as the critical resource allocation and management tool in state government, plodding along unglamorously but surely, impervious, it seems, to significant change. And the process followed in developing the budget most likely continues to be largely incremental in nature, constituting another possible impediment to change in the management of state government.

The successful application of strategic planning in state government depends on fully understanding and creatively using the budgeting process. If ignored, not only will budgeting not go away, it will surely carry the day, making long-range planning at best considerably less productive, at worst totally ineffective. Of very special interest in the context of this book is the Federal government's experience with the Planning, Programming, Budgeting System (PPBS). There are valuable lessons to be learned about both innovation in the public sector generally and the traditional budget process.

The incremental approach to budget making, disdained by some and welcomed by others as a bulwark holding back hordes of long-range planning fanatics, by definition focuses attention on proposed increases in line-item spending by operating agencies, accepting as largely unquestioned the prior period's allocation. A 1971 study confirmed that incremental budgeting was in wide use, based on the fact that states tended to remain in the same position relative to other states in terms of spending, and there is no good evidence to show that the incremental approach has declined appreciably up to the present. A significant trait of this kind of budgeting is its reliance on line agency initiative and the concomitant weak role of the Governor in policy formulation. The process is, thus, notoriously hostile toward innovation.[12]

The popularity of incremental budget building is easily understandable. It is, very simply, easy to do. The issues are certainly less complex than those that would surface in digging below the baseline budget, and the consequent time devoted to fact gathering and analysis is much less. And, of course, dealing solely with the increments avoids political controversy. Unfortunately for those who have invested heavily in learning the ins and outs of the incremental approach, it is woefully inadequate for the new era of no-growth and even relative decline in the resources available to government. The choice of which budget receives how much of an increase over the prior year is fundamentally different from deciding which budget receives how much less than last year; or, even more perplexing, which program is decimated so that one judged of greater worth can continue. The hard choices and trade-offs that will characterize planning and budgeting for the foreseeable future cannot conceivably be made through the traditional incremental process, which possesses no pertinent logic to apply in this new situation. This is not, however, to say that politics and bargaining, human intuition and judgment will be less important in the budget allocation process. The point is that the vehicle by which the decisions are made is no longer adequate.

It is likely that "the times" have long demanded a firmer policy context within which the incremental budgeting process can work effectively. This has been recognized by the growing evidence of sunset legislation as a signal of perceived need. A process that is aimed at getting through on a day-to-day basis without serious political confrontation or controversy may mask issues of vital strategic importance that need to be resolved *now* in order to avert adverse consequences in the future. It does appear somewhat ironic that some older industrial cities in the Northeast and Midwest are just lately discovering the need for longer-range, more comprehensive planning after all of the adverse consequences have occurred. It may not be too late to rebuild the cities, but it will surely be much more costly than strategies aimed at forestalling those consequences would have been. The rebuilding job is incredibly more difficult now that it must proceed on a much diminished resource base. The fact is, the incremental approach to annual planning and budgeting failed to surface the critical issues, despite the recognizable portents of decline.

The last major innovation to be implemented in governmental budgeting was the introduction of the executive budget, prepared by the executive departments and submitted to the legislature by the chief executive after appropriate revision and consolidation. A brief flirtation with so-called "performance" budgeting—by major work functions and activities—failed to have widespread and lasting impact, although it stimulated a variety of productivity improvement projects at the local level, which have surely had some positive impact. The next major attempt at innovation in budgeting, PPBS, merits more serious attention in this discussion, principally because its dramatic demise has been used by many to impugn the efficacy of long-range planning.

The PPBS experiment was a forthright attempt to reform the Federal budget process, and its failure is probably due, in large measure, to underestimation of the strength of traditional budgeting. What PPBS attempted to do, according to a knowledgeable observer, was to "recast federal budgeting from a repetitive process for financing permanent bureaucracies into an instrument for deciding the purposes and programs of government." The purpose of analysis, according to this observer, was to serve budget decision making, not to be an end in itself. The downfall of PPBS lay in its failure to "penetrate the vital routines of putting together and justifying a budget. Always separate but never equal, the analysts had little influence over the form or content of the budget."[13]

There are a variety of possible reasons why PPBS failed to make a lasting impact on the Federal budget process. It has been suggested that PPBS was far too cumbersome, requiring the handling of an inordinate amount of paper, that it was implemented without properly taking into account the unique circumstances of the different departments, that the Bureau of the Budget was not committed to change and thus did not use the results of PPBS analysis, and that the support staff assigned to PPBS were too few for the immense task.[14] Generally speaking, what was at work was the all too common attempt to accomplish too much, too fast, coupled with the failure to commit enough resources to do the job adequately.

A convincing case can be made for the position that the kind of policy analysis that PPBS was presumably capable of generating was sorely needed in the Federal government, whether a strong constituency supported it or not. Now that a sweeping move to reduce the size of the government is underway, the absence of goals, priorities, and strategies appears much more telling. As one author has noted, "It is indeed difficult to see how either advocacy planning (with its heavy burden of special advantages) or incrementalism (with its heavy burden of outdated programs) can provide, within viable budget limits, the new policy initiatives needed to solve our great advocacy socioeconomic problems."[15]

Over the past few years, a halfway house of sorts, usually called "policy analysis," has developed. There appears to be no universally accepted definition of the technique, although it falls short of formal, comprehensive long-range planning. It appears basically to consist of the application of available analytical techniques to the analysis of specific policy issues. In a 1979 symposium on policy analysis in government, it is described as "an applied discipline which relies heavily on understanding the techniques drawn from other scientific disciplines such as economics, statistics, political science, applied mathematics, sociology, and public administration."[16] It is usually closely tied to the budgeting process, and has been said to encompass such systems as PPBS and Zero Based Budgeting (a variant of PPBS). One observer has unflatteringly described policy analysis in practice as "social science opportunistically applied to the issues of the day" and has pointed out its lack of "central focus."[17]

There is evidence that policy analysis techniques have been applied in several, if not most, states, and there is no reason to doubt that they have contributed to more reasoned and rational decisions.[18] The focus on specific issues or programs, however, and the absence of a rigorous process hardly qualify policy analysis to meet the pressing need for governments to set priorities and to make painful choices among broad courses of action.

Government and Business: How Different?

There are several obvious differences between the public and for-profit sectors that must be taken into consideration in determining how best to apply strategic planning in state government, and certain of the major ones will be reviewed briefly below. It is easier to identify these differences than to assess their significance. In fact, many of the more popular distinctions have become enshrined in the conventional wisdom on the slimmest of scientific evidence. As a recent study of strategic management in the non-profit sector observes, "Although some would argue that the management of not-for-profit organizations is significantly different than the management of profit organizations because of differing organizational characteristics, there are few or no major studies indicating that this is the case." The study goes on to point out that certain characteristics of non-profit organizations that seem to cause unusual managerial problems also appear "to a greater or lesser extent" in for-profit entities.[19]

Much of the large body of conventional wisdom about public-private sector differences has resulted from brief forays of businesspeople into government, or at least from sustained contact—long enough to be frustrating but too brief for in-depth understanding. The strange, indeed alien, environment of government can cause a "culture shock" of sorts that impedes learning. As Peter Drucker so eloquently points out, the oft-heard cry that not-for-profit institutions should be more "businesslike" in their management reveals a shallow understanding of the dynamics of non-profit sector management. The fact is, it makes little sense to ascribe governmental shortcomings to their not behaving like businesses, which they are clearly not. "Businesslike" as applied to government normally is understood as efficiency, when, Drucker observes, the overriding concern is effectiveness.[20]

There is also reason to believe that the distinctions that do exist are blurring and that the similarities are becoming more obvious, at least insofar as large-scale organizations are concerned.[21] Certainly the gray area appears to be expanding, witness the many public-private sector cooperative projects that have been initiated throughout the country over the past few years in such areas as economic development, employment and training, and management improvement in government. Another signal of the blurring boundaries is the growing popularity of public management graduate education within schools of business, rather than "pure" public administration education.

The foregoing points are not intended to downplay the need to consider explicitly the special features of the public environment when engaging in the transfer of technologies or techniques from the for-profit sector. Anyone doubting the immensity of the challenge, intellectually and emotionally, need only read former Secretary of the Treasury Blumenthal's "Candid Reflections," which provides a sobering account of the difficulties. Although his plaintive account of trials and tribulations at times seems unduly defensive and self-pitying, it is instructive that a person of such obvious commitment and capability found the going so rough.[22] Again, it is easy enough to recite the differences; the challenge is to put them into realistic perspective, separating out the more fundamental from the merely operational, and to assess the practical impact of the differences. The major distinctions that we will review are considered as complexities to be understood and mastered, rather than as insurmountable hurdles, or excuses for non-performance.[23]

Purposes and Ends: "The Bottom Line"

Perhaps the most fundamental difference between the two sectors lies in the realm of purpose and ultimate ends. Although both business and government provide products and services to customers who must ultimately be satisfied, the so-called "bottom line" for business—the generation of profits—obviously does not exist where governmental services are concerned. Therefore, government must implement its programs without the benefit of an immediate objective measure of the success of its management. There is no question but that a powerful method of self-discipline is thus absent in the public sector. As Drucker has pointed out, in the for-profit sector, "satisfaction of the customer is . . . the basis for assuring performance and results in a business." By contrast, the "customers" of government must register their approval or disapproval much less directly because governments are paid out of general budget allocations that are only very indirectly tied to results and performance, save for the sobering results of elections.[24]

Short of attempting to establish the profit motive in the delivery of public services, an approach shown by recent attempts to "privatize" some municipal services, the next best solution to the problem of effectiveness measurement is to formulate specific standards of performance within programs. Granted, the discipline of the ultimate "bottom line" will be missing, but better to build this halfway house than to assume that governmental performance necessarily defies measurement. It is in the area of estimating the cost of governmental services, of efficiency, that the absence of the profit standard will be most sorely missed, for only through variations in profit is it possible to determine whether goods and services are priced appropriately.

Formulation of Policy

There is no question that the policy formulation and ratification process is, in a number of respects, considerably more complex in government than in business. As former Secretary Blumenthal expressed it, "To control the development of a policy, to shape out of that cacophony of divergent interests and dissonant voices an approach that eventually leads to a consensus and can be administered in a coherent fashion is an entirely different task in the government than it is for the chief executive of a company."[25]

The problem is not that public policies are more difficult to formulate in a conceptual or technical sense; it is, rather, that the ratification process permits many more "fingers in the pie." Indeed, one of our democratic tenets is that policies should not be too easy to make, and our national and state government structures reflect this philosophical bias. Corporate boards traditionally have little in common with governmental legislative bodies. Whereas the directors of a corporation basically represent top management, including those in the organization being governed, and tend to identify with the interest of the whole corporation, legislators in government not only represent relatively narrow constituencies, but also view their proper role as adversarial and often antagonistic to the aims of the executive branch. And to this must be added the myriad of special interests engaged in lobbying for or against specific policies and the electoral politicking that tends to distort the pros and cons associated with particular policies and to work against comprehensive consideration of issues.

Whether the democratic ideal of checks and balances should be sacrificed in some way to achieve more expeditious policy making is beyond the ken of this inquiry. Rather, it is assumed that the real challenge is to achieve effective and timely policy making within the traditional democratic constraints. In this regard, it must be pointed out that throughout the history of this republic, major—at times radical—policies have been successfully implemented at the national and state levels, often with astounding speed. The New Deal of the 1930s is only one of the more dramatic examples. Two elements appear essential for the rapid implementation of policies that represent dramatic departures from current practice: external events of a crisis nature and a strong chief executive able and willing to communicate effectively to the people at large.

A final observation on this topic is the growing complexity of policy making in the corporate sphere as the pressure has mounted for business to take social concerns into account when formulating policies. Not only have governmental regulations complicated the life of business, but also the activities of consumer groups and even the increasing representation of "outside" interests on boards of directors. Business has always relied on strong chief executives to keep the policy-making process going, and external crises have often been necessary to jolt large for-profit organizations out of established courses of action. Witness the late awakening of the American auto industry to the need to compete with the highly effective Japanese and other foreign auto industries. Thus, it is possible to conclude that, while the public sector is responding to demands for improved effectiveness, which have prompted consideration of such business techniques as strategic planning, the private sector has come under increasing pressure to demonstrate concern for the broader effects of its internal decision making.

Influence of the Chief Executive

As Blumenthal found at the Treasury Department, the chief executive in the public sector has less latitude in exercising leadership than his or her peer on the for-profit side. The adversarial relationship with the legislature is a severe constraint on the use of power, as is the relative lack of influence over a bureaucracy protected by the civil service system. The nature of the role of the governmental chief executive also forces the allocation of tremendous time to political concerns, including explaining and selling proposed policies to the electorate at large. Although an indispensable part of the public chief executive's work, this need to justify policies to a large and diverse citizenry is not notable for bringing to light a full explication of the pros and cons; rather, it tends to promote gross oversimplification and hyperbole. In addition, the lack of the ultimate "bottom line" measurement of performance can lead to an inordinate focus on appearance; as Blumenthal noted, "That is why you can be successful if you appear to be successful," although he added that other factors also figured into success.[26]

Human Resource Management

Nothing definitive can be ventured about the overall differences in capability between public and for-profit managers. Throughout American history, certainly, politics and public service have attracted scores of outstanding citizens, including top business leaders. If there has ever been a significant capability gap between the two sectors at the lower- and mid-management levels, then it has most likely diminished appreciably as governmental compensation levels have approached the business standard.

There are, however, some significant systemic differences. Continuity of top management is one of the most apparent and serious; not only do public chief executives come and go with relative frequency as their electoral fortunes wax and wane, but perhaps more importantly, whole second, and sometimes third, echelons of management change with them. While this affords an opportunity for redirecting the government in concert with a new electoral mandate, the lack of transition mechanisms and experienced persons to take the reins of departmental directorship conspire to deny this possible benefit. It is inconceivable that organizational continuity can be maintained through such upheavals, and the amount of "starting all over again" must be quite large.

It is not being suggested that the solution to the problem of a lack of management continuity is the carte blanche extension of civil service protection upward into the "political" levels of the bureaucracy. Indeed, such a cure might be worse than the original malady. The point is that continuity is frequently lacking, and the problem does need to be addressed. Answers may be found in a variety of approaches, including more detailed planning for the transition from one administration to another and the implementation of in-depth management development programs (in contrast to the casual and irregular use of training seminars). Ideally, a kind of public service tradition is the goal, rather than merely the enhancement of job security.

Lack of flexibility in hiring, firing, and promoting personnel is a commonly cited characteristic of the public sector that distinguishes it from business, although there is no convincing evidence that would indicate the importance of the distinction. Probably more important is the lack of well planned and financed staff development programs in the public sector. There are certainly few if any counterparts in government to the meticulous grooming of managers for leadership on the for-profit side.

Modern Management Techniques and Technology

Government has clearly lagged in the application of modern management principles and techniques, and it is likely that the states have been especially remiss in utilizing advances in the art of management. This may be partly because of the high cost of such modern management tools as the computer and to sincere questions about how to adapt largely for-profit sector developments for the public context. It seems fair to conclude that a major reason is likely to be the skepticism, and even cynicism, bred by poorly conceived and executed management improvement efforts, such as the PPBS effort at the Federal level. The cause of long-range planning was probably seriously set back by this and other naive attempts to realize overnight blessings at minimal cost.

Implications

None of the distinctions discussed above, taken together, make a compelling case against the application of strategic planning in state government. The experience of the for-profit sector, however, must be applied with great caution in government, making a conscious effort to adapt the experience to the unique characteristics of the states.

The following general, somewhat rough guidelines are

addressed in greater detail in the following chapter, which focuses on the design and implementation of strategic planning processes in state government:

☐ The Governor must be personally convinced of the essential value of strategic planning and serve as focal point of any strategic planning effort; he or she must be involved intensively from the start in both the design and implementation phases. It is strongly advisable that the Governor's expectations as to the results to be achieved through strategic planning, as well as the acceptable level of costs, be clarified early in the design of the state's planning program and reflected in the ultimate design.

☐ The Governor will assume a critical political leadership and consensus-building role in undertaking a strategic planning effort, if it is to have a fair chance of succeeding. At the appropriate times, the state's managers and its legislators will need to be oriented as to the costs and benefits of the planning initiative, along with the major technical steps involved, and the Governor's personal participation in this educational effort will be crucial.

☐ It is important that the various options for applying strategic planning be explicitly considered in formulating a planning effort tailored to the particular needs and characteristics of a given state government. It would be a serious mistake to assume that the only available course of action is to implement a formal, comprehensive "system" involving all state executive departments. Given the mixed results realized thus far in long-range planning in the public sector, and the highly visible failure of PPBS at the Federal level, a Governor and his cabinet might be well advised to take a paced, incremental approach, pilot testing the design before launching a larger, higher profile effort.

☐ It might also be advisable initially to avoid attempting to establish too close a link to the annual or biennial budgetary process. Although there must eventually be a very explicit linkage if state goals and strategies are to be implemented in a timely fashion, the complexities involved in impacting this traditional, well-entrenched management process argue against taking on too much early in strategic planning. It is also important to keep in mind that the positive impacts of strategic planning are not realized solely through the budgetary process; there are many ways to advance strategies once they have been formulated. For example, Governors can shape program directions through the appointment of departmental directors, and tax and regulatory policies represent powerful levers for change. The focus in this book on the budget reflects not only that it is the single most important lever for change, but also that the link between it and the planning process is more often than not highly tenuous.

☐ Finally, the expert advice and guidance of business executives with in-depth experience in strategic planning might be a valuable tactic to employ in both the design and implementation phases of strategic planning. Of course, care must be taken in selecting and using private sector resources. The Governor will want the assistance only of those who are committed to the enhancement of the strategic capability of government and who are sensitive to and respect the distinctions between the two sectors. In addition, the executives who are called upon to serve in this advisory capacity must have the will and patience to learn the dynamics of governmental organization and decision making if their advice is to be truly useful.

To Plan or Not:
Is There a Realistic Choice?

Thus far, the emphasis has been on examining the process of strategic planning, the lessons learned through its application in business, the planning foundation that has been built in state government, and the unique characteristics of the governmental sector that need to be understood and factored explicitly into a state's planning program. It has been suggested that, while the business experience must be adapted to the state context, there are no insurmountable barriers to the successful use of strategic planning in state government. In the introduction to this chapter, it is pointed out that the present time is auspicious for the application of this powerful new management tool by the states for a number of reasons, including the abundant knowledge acquired through business applications, the increasingly rich theoretical base, and the swing of the pendulum toward the states while a conscious reductionist philosophy is applied in the Federal government. In bringing this chapter to a close, we think it useful to return briefly to the question of why strategic planning should be applied by the states, as opposed to the question of whether it can be.

The critical question is whether state government can afford not to utilize strategic planning in some form as we move further into an era of relative economic stasis, when citizens doubt the effectiveness of government, and the revenues in most states are inadequate. State planning, indeed all governmental planning up to now, has been closely tied to the incremental budgeting process and hence well adapted to a situation of continuous, at least modest, growth. Making tough choices is not characteristic in this resource allocation environment, and the inevitable bargaining and trading-off has typically allowed all major actors to "win" something.

The challenge increasingly is to decide what cuts to make in state budgets, and the constraints—fiscally and politically—are so severe that budget reductions will be deep and certain programs will accordingly suffer, if not disappear. The traditional budget process offers scant help in such a situation, which demands that the choices be identified, understood, and evaluated. Merely imposing across-the-board budget reductions, although they may for a time be politically appealing, is a strikingly irrational solution, acknowledging that there are no priorities.

Whatever its limitations in practice, strategic planning does offer an extensively tested approach to identifying and making the fundamental choices. It does offer a hope for rationality in a time of turbulence and seemingly constant crises, when the pressure is to trim budgets mindlessly. The problem is not a lack of specific programmatic options; as Harold Hovey and David Hartley have demonstrated so well for the Council of State Planning Agencies in the areas of urban development and economic policy, respectively, states have an impressive array of tools at their command once overall directions have been determined.[27] But how does the Governor, and ultimately the legislature, choose among the variety of strategies available to the states? It is here that a different planning approach is essential.

Certain other characteristics of strategic planning make it uniquely appropriate for the times:

☐ It is flexible, in that it can be applied in a variety of ways with differing resource commitments, either for all of state government in a comprehensive planning system approach, or more narrowly for a particular issue area. There is no imperative, furthermore, that existing planning be discontinued in order to apply strategic planning, although procedural revisions may be necessary and linkages will be in order.
☐ It is action-oriented in that its focus is the chief executive's need to make the truly strategic decisions in a timely manner.
☐ It provides conscious attention to the cost of implementation and organizational structure requirements so as to ensure that economy, efficiency, and productivity will be explicit considerations in the strategy formulation process.

The "bottom line" for Governors, state managers, and legislators is that strategic planning provides a framework for defining the key decisions affecting the long-term future of the states and for making those decisions with an eye to outcomes, long-term costs, and the steps required in implementation.

CHAPTER II NOTES

1. Robert D. Behn, "Leadership for Cut-Back Management: The Use of Corporate Strategy," *Public Administration Review* (November–December 1980): 617.

2. The Research Group, *The Legal Basis for State Policy Planning* (Washington, D.C.: Council of State Planning Agencies, 1977), p. 9. See also, Harold F. Wise, *History of State Planning—an Interpretive Commentary* (Washington, D.C.: Council of State Planning Agencies, 1977), pp. 8–13.

3. Wise, *History*, pp. 14–20.

4. Ibid.

5. Ibid., p. 22. See also, The Research Group, *Legal Basis*, pp. 5–9; and Leonard V. Wilson and L. V. Watkins, "State Planning: Problems and Promises," *State Government* 48 (Autumn 1979): 242–243.

6. Thad L. Beyle and Deil S. Wright, "The Governor, Planning, and Governmental Activity," in *The American Governor in Behavioral Perspective*, ed. Thad L. Beyle and J. Oliver Williams (New York: Harper and Row, 1972), pp. 196–197.

7. The Research Group, *Legal Basis*, pp. 16–18.

8. Wise, *History*, p. 27.

9. Cogan and Associates, *Statewide Policy Instruments* (Washington, D.C.: Council of State Planning Agencies, 1977), pp. 14–17.

10. Charles P. Warren, *The States and Urban Strategies: A Comparative Analysis* (Washington, D.C.: National Academy of Public Administration, 1980), p. 50.

11. Lynn Muchmore, *Evaluation of State Planning* (Washington, D.C.: Council of State Planning Agencies, 1977), pp. 3–7.

12. Ira Sharkansky, "State Administrators in the Political Process," in *Politics in the American States: A Comparative Analysis*, ed. Herbert Jacob and Kenneth N. Vines (Boston: Little, Brown and Company, Inc., 1971), pp. 255–260.

13. Allen Schick, "A Death in the Bureaucracy: The Demise of Federal PPB," *Public Administration Review* 33 (March–April 1973): 146–156. See also, Allen Schick, *Budget Innovation in the States* (Washington, D.C.: The Brookings Institution, 1971), pp. 103–105.

14. Schick, "A Death," pp. 146–156.

15. Robert B. Buchele, *The Management of Business and Public Organizations* (New York: McGraw-Hill, Inc., 1977), p. 119. See also, Behn, "Leadership for Cut-Back Management."

16. Mark Schneider and David Swinton, Introduction to "A Symposium:

Policy Analysis in State and Local Government," *Public Administration Review* 39 (January–February 1979): 13.

17. Allen Schick, "Beyond Analysis," *Public Administration Review* 37 (May–June 1977): 261.

18. Selma J. Mushkin, "Policy Analysis in State and Community," *Public Administration Review* 37 (May–June 1977): 245–246.

19. Max S. Wortman, Jr., "Strategic Management: Not-for-Profit Organizations," in Schendel and Hofer, pp. 353–354. See also, Michael A. Murray, "Comparing Public and Private Management: An Exploratory Essay," *Public Administration Review* 35 (July–August 1975): 370.

20. Peter F. Drucker, *Management: Tasks, Responsibilities, Practices* (New York: Harper and Row, 1973), pp. 137–138.

21. Charles E. Summer, *Strategic Behavior in Business and Government* (Boston: Little, Brown and Company, 1980), p. 33.

22. Michael Blumenthal, "Candid Reflections of a Businessman in Washington," *Fortune* 99 (January 29, 1979): 36–49.

23. The following sources were most useful in selecting the distinctions to be discussed: (1) Blumenthal, "Candid Reflections." (2) Joseph L. Bower, "Effective Public Management," *Harvard Business Review* 55 (March–April 1977): 131–140. (3) Drucker, *Management*. (4) Michael H. Moskow, *Strategic Planning in Business and Government* (New York: Committee for Economic Development, 1978), pp. 26–35. (5) Steiner and Miner, *Management Policy*, pp. 757–771. (6) Murray Weidenbaum and Linda Rockwood, "Corporate Planning Versus Government Planning," *The Public Interest* (Winter 1977): 59–72.

24. Drucker, *Management*, pp. 141–142.

25. Blumenthal, "Candid Reflections," p. 44.

26. Ibid., p. 36.

27. Harold A. Hovey, *State Urban Development Strategies* (Washington, D.C.: Council of State Planning Agencies, 1977); and David K. Hartley, *State Strategies for National Economic Policy* (Washington, D.C.: Council of State Planning Agencies, 1977).

CHAPTER III

Approaches
to Implementation:
Some Practical Guidance

Introduction

IIII▶ The previous two chapters have provided an introduction to the theory and practice of strategic planning and have examined those features of the public sector, and especially state government, that deserve particular attention in developing a strategic planning program. The major aim of this chapter is to provide Governors, state managers, and legislators with practical guidance in the implementation of strategic planning. First the basic steps involved in designing a strategic planning program in state government are described. Next, the broad options available in terms of scope and depth regarding applying strategic planning in state government are examined, and a general course of action is suggested. Finally, the reader is provided with an illustration of how the application of strategic planning might proceed.

The point has been made more than once that each individual state will require a strategic planning program specifically tailored to its particular characteristics and situation. Some states are attempting to cope with rapid growth, more are preoccupied with what has been called the "management of decline." Some states have substantial experience in formal long-range planning while others have focused almost entirely on annual or biennial budget planning. Certain Governors understand and are strongly committed to long-range planning; others bring less experience and greater doubts as to its efficacy. There is, then, no average state to which this book can be directed in any meaningful sense, and the most that can be offered is a framework within which detailed strategic planning programs can be formulated.

The Gubernatorial Commitment to Proceed

The most critical element in the success of strategic planning is the understanding and active support and participation of the state's chief executive officer. In chapter 1, it was noted that managers frequently adopt a stance of watchful waiting, reserving their commitment to the process of planning or to implementation of a completed plan until the position of the chief executive is demonstrated by behavior, rather than mere exhortation. Serious doubt about the priority accorded planning by the chief executive, fostered, say, by the failure to commit substantial time to the review of plans, can be a tremendous impediment to the formulation or implementation of a planning process. The Governor not only ensures that an adequate process and structure for planning are in place, but also that the requisite resources are allocated and a favorable climate for planning is created.

In light of the very central role of the Governor in the strategic planning process, it is appropriate that the exploration of planning options and formulation of a recommended strategic planning program for the state be undertaken only after securing the explicit commitment of the Governor to such developmental activities. This preliminary commitment to consider strategic planning might consist of the following major elements:

☐ A clear understanding of the strategic planning process, including not only the potential benefits to the particular state but also the limitations of such planning and the associated costs.
☐ A firm grasp of the substantial personal commitment required of the Governor if strategic planning is to be

successful, including reviewing and acting on the plans that the process generates.

☐ Authorization to proceed with the development of the "plan to plan," involving the planning audit, the formulation of planning objectives, and the design of a planning process and structure.

☐ The designation of a senior executive to provide leadership to this first, pre-strategic planning phase.

Such commitment to examine strategic planning in detail might be secured in a meeting of the Governor, the state planning director, and senior members of the Governor's personal staff. The commitment is likely to be firmer if preparation for such a meeting includes the development of a detailed memorandum addressing the points previously set forth. The memorandum should convey clearly the potential contribution of strategic planning to the Governor's articulated administration goals, while also making clear that the benefits will be realized only at a significant cost in gubernatorial time and managerial involvement (see Appendix A). The Governor should understand that the only commitment being requested at this stage is to explore the options for applying strategic planning and to formulate a planning program, which will be explicitly approved by the Governor before being undertaken.

If in this meeting any serious gap in the Governor's understanding of strategic planning, in terms of process, potential benefits, or limitations, is revealed, it would be unwise to proceed further before the gap is closed. Once it becomes known that the application of strategic planning is being seriously considered in the state, resistance is likely to build rapidly and the Governor will be closely watched to determine the depth of commitment. It is not inconceivable that resistance will be strengthened, and the ultimate planning initiative weakened, if the Governor inadvertently discloses a lack of conviction or understanding of the strategic planning process. It is also important, in order to avoid prematurely damaging the credibility of the upcoming planning initiative, that the person whom the Governor entrusts with the responsibility to develop the strategic planning program is not only a close and trusted associate of the Governor, with easy access, but also is open to the application of new techniques and processes. The person need not be a strong advocate of long-range planning, and certainly should not be an uncritical admirer, but he or she should not harbor ingrained prejudice against planning. The point is to ensure that the Governor receives as objective an analysis of the possibilities for applying strategic planning as is possible given the time available.

It may prove useful at this early stage of development for the Governor to designate a small strategic planning steering committee, consisting of those senior officials involved in the preliminary commitment session, with the charge of assisting in exploring the options and formulating a recommended course of action. Such a body might ensure fuller consideration of options; diverse perspectives on such a complex matter cannot help but be useful. It might also be a means of building the support of persons whose leadership during the planning process will be essential.

The Planning Audit

It would seem to go without saying that no organization should proceed with the detailed design of a new planning process without first having gained a complete understanding of its planning requirements, as well as the strengths and shortcomings of existing planning activities. However, it is likely that this essential step in the design process is frequently either glossed over or even entirely omitted in the rush to demonstrate a commitment to modern management techniques. The basic purpose of the planning audit is to assess the planning requirements of the state and the status of current state planning. Not only is it important to know whether, and to what extent, strategic planning requirements are being satisfied, but also to understand the status of shorter-range planning, particularly the budget preparation process. In keeping with the principle of "first things first," it may very well be unwise for a state to launch a wide-range strategic planning effort on the foundation of a poorly conceived or inadequately documented budget preparation process. At the least, such a situation would call for scaling down the broader effort and living with incremental progress while firming up the foundation.

The steps involved in the planning audit will now be described in some detail. It should be noted by way of introduction that the audit may be as intensive and time-consuming as the circumstances of a particular state warrant. An exhaustive review of planning in even a small state might consume four to six months of the time of two or three senior staff analysts. The only guidance that can be offered with any certainty is that the more complete the understanding of planning needs, the better the ultimate planning design is likely to be. It is likely that the Governor should plan on the full-time involvement of at least one senior analyst for a period of three months, in order to ensure a firm enough grasp of the situation to proceed with a detailed design.

The specific methods employed in gathering the information required by the audit will vary from state to state, depending on the volume and the unique problems associated with fact gathering. In some states, much of the information may be available through the central planning office; in others, several different departments may be the repositories of needed information. The specific circumstances will dictate the balance among such techniques as personal interviewing, review of documentation, and the administration of written questionnaires.

The first step in the planning audit is to determine the planning needs and requirements of the Governor. This might be accomplished most effectively through one or two lengthy interviews that are formal and structured to the extent that a schedule of specific questions has been developed in advance (see Appendix B). It would be useful to share the questions with the Governor prior to the session. A primary outcome of this step will be the clarification of the Governor's expectations about planning and his or her planning philosophy. One of the most important factors to be considered in designing a planning process is the use to which the chief executive intends to put planning. It is essential to understand whether the Governor prefers to focus on short-term operational issues and has little interest in, or understanding of, long-range planning, or, at the other pole, is comfortable with a longer time horizon and prefers to exert influence over the course of future events through formal long-range planning. This is not to say that there may not be considerable subjectivity in the pinning down of a planned philosophy, or that a Governor's philosophy may not change significantly over time; it is merely to say that the Governor's current expectations and biases about long-range planning must be explicitly factored into the design of a planning program if it is to be realistic, whether the Governor's attitudes function as a constraint to be overcome or as tremendous motivating force.

The extent to which this in-depth interview with the Governor should focus on his or her satisfaction with current state planning will depend on the chief executive's familiarity with the state's planning practices. The perspective of a newly elected Governor will obviously be different from that of a chief executive beginning a second term. Depending on the level of familiarity, it is useful to gain a sense of what the Governor considers the major shortcomings of current state planning processes; even prior to that, to determine what the Governor sees as the major elements of planning as practiced by the state government.

It is also important to clarify those broad issues on which the Governor prefers to focus over the long run because such information will be critical in the selective application of strategic planning if something less than a government-wide planning initiative is undertaken. Even though there may be one or more formal statements of gubernatorial priorities, goals, or objectives in existence, it is advisable to confirm directions at this point. Also, of course, extant documentation may be too general–of the "apple pie and motherhood" variety—or too encompassing, constituting the proverbial endless litany of good intentions. What is needed is a limited set of issues that are of high priority to the Governor in the sense that they have a preeminent claim on gubernatorial time. This facet of the interview should also shed light on the Governor's philosophy. In discussing the highest priority issues, it should be possible to understand more firmly whether the Governor is most interested in achieving greater short-term management control or in the broader consideration of alternative strategies to be employed over the longer run.

It is essential that complete notes of the interview(s) with the Governor be recorded and prepared in finished, edited form. Such notes will indicate areas needing to be explored in subsequent interviews. Also, through his or her review and sign-off on the interview record, the Governor will have an opportunity to clarify and firm up key points.

The next step in the planning audit is to inventory formal planning requirements in force in state government. What kinds of planning processes and documentation are required by state legislation? What Federal planning requirements are being imposed through grants-in-aid or other mechanisms?

The third step is to survey the planning activity currently taking place throughout the government. The cost in time of an in-depth comprehensive survey is likely to be prohibitive in light of the projected benefits, and so substantial selectivity will be required. Basically, the wider the scope (in terms of breadth of impact or substantive area) or departmental involvement in a particular planning process, the more detailed the attention it should receive in the survey. Applying this yardstick, the survey would devote greater attention to existing "master planning" activities than to the planning required by specific Federal grant programs. The annual or biennial budget-related planning also would receive detailed attention because it is an activity common to all state agencies.

The survey should focus on the following elements of every planning activity covered:

☐ Stated purposes.
☐ Scope, in terms of substantive area (e.g., health, economic development), client group affected, and time frame (encompassing one, two, five, or more years hence).

☐ The main steps in the planning process and the chronology.
☐ The nature of the planning products generated by the process. (Statements of priorities, goals, objectives? Detailed program plans with deadlines?)
☐ Any formal or informal means in operation for coordinating or integrating planning processes.

The foregoing elements can be described without involving evaluative judgments. To make the survey of real use in designing a strategic planning program will, however, require going beyond objective description of the different planning processes being used in the state. The basic concern is to gain some understanding of the effectiveness of the various processes, and the most practical approach to the question, given realistic time constraints, is most likely the solicitation of opinion, by way of personal interviews and questionnaires, from senior managers with substantial experience in using the particular processes. It is relevant to know whether those who do the planning and use the resulting plans consider them effective in terms of achieving the stated purposes and relevant in terms of assisting them in doing their jobs. Do managers believe that particular plans exercise influence on their activities, or are they merely produced in response to external requirements and rarely, if ever, consulted once completed? It is also important to understand what managers consider the shortcomings of the planning processes that they use and the possible remedies.

From the foregoing survey should emerge a relatively complete picture of the planning currently being done in the state, the subject matters, aims, processes, and interrelationships, and a sense of the effectiveness of the different processes, based on the testimony of experienced managers. The detail will, to be sure, be uneven and the assessment of effectiveness subjective, but even this less-than-complete understanding of the state's planning environment is preferable to proceeding blindly with the design of a strategic planning program, based on the general assumption that it is needed. The information yielded will prove valuable in a number of respects.

☐ There will be a rough comprehension of the amount of time being spent on all kinds of planning, and this can be taken into account in formulating a strategic planning strategy. If considerable managerial time is already being spent on planning of one kind or another, then it may be desirable to pace the implementation of strategic planning so as not to place too great a burden on those doing the planning. The pace might gradually increase as other planning requirements are obviated.

☐ There will be a sense of the attitudes of experienced and senior managers toward planning, and therefore a better idea of the challenge involved in creating a positive planning climate in the government.

☐ The depth of the foundation for long-range planning will be clearer and can be factored into the design of the strategic planning program. As has been observed earlier, the finding that annual or biennial budget-related planning is poorly documented and/or exerts little real influence on the allocation of resources indicates that a tenuous foundation may exist for longer-range planning, and so the strategic planning initiative might best be deferred, or at least undertaken in a more incremental fashion.

☐ The extent to which long-range issues are being grappled with currently will be clearer, thus demonstrating the need for the application of a new approach to long-range planning in the government.

The legislative dimension of state planning must be examined as part of the planning audit, even though direct consultation with legislators at this very early stage in strategic planning might do more harm than good through premature public, and hence political, attention. The strategic planning program might, indeed, be short-lived if it became a political issue before having been developed in detail. At this point in the design process, it might suffice to pinpoint the interfaces of the current planning processes with the legislative process (e.g., what budget-related planning documentation is sent to what legislative committees, when, and how is it acted upon?) and to clarify the committee and subcommittee structure involved in planning. Of course, whether the legislature should be at arms length at this point depends on the circumstances in the particular state. It is conceivable that personal legislative involvement at this stage could be very useful when, for instance, a strong positive tie exists between the Governor and a legislative leadership that is interested in the improvement of state management. Such involvement would be especially compelling if one or more legislative committees were already active in a positive, constructive sense in some facet of state long-range planning.

The management dimension is also relevant to the design question. For example, is there a budget control system that provides managers with regular reports enabling them to compare actual to budgeted expenditures and that requires budget approval for expenditures? Is the budget control system based solely on object-of-expenditure tracking, or are expenditures controlled on a project, activity, or program basis as well? What is the research capability of the state government? Is there a unit engaged in some kind of environmental scanning and forecasting? What is the computing capability, if any? The point is to assess roughly those facets of the state's management infrastructure that are so obviously underdeveloped that they represent a serious constraint on any strategic planning effort. The specific impact and required remedial effort cannot be determined until a definite strategic planning option is being examined.

Another dimension to be considered as part of the planning audit is the level of staff effort being devoted to "pure" planning activities: the kinds and numbers of personnel whose primary responsibility is the formulation of plans or the provision of direct support to managers in planning. The cadre of professional planners in state government represents a potentially rich resource to be tapped in implementing a strategic planning program. At the best, their active support and cooperation can be enlisted in the strategic planning effort. At the least, their neutrality can be sought. To give short shrift to the need to identify and utilize this resource would be counter-productive indeed. Long-range planning is difficult to do in the best of times and represents an awesome challenge when economic vicissitudes focus attention on the immed-iate task of keeping the annual or biennial budget in balance. Properly motivated and channeled, professional planners might provide the zeal and determination re-quired to support an ambitious strategic planning effort. This is not to say that the commitment of the general manager is not critical to the success of any planning endeavor; nor is it to deny that the enthusiasm of profes-sional planners must be tempered and restrained so as not to lose touch with the realities of day-to-day management. But the fact remains that there is a great need for hard-core loyalists who are committed to the extension of plan-ning in state government and who can be counted on for constant support. The earlier they are apprised of the stra-tegic planning program and asked to share their knowledge and experience in shaping it, the smoother the implemen-tation process is apt to be.

Review of the Strategic Planning Options

Three broad approaches to the application of strategic planning are available to Governors. They are by no means mutually exclusive, and it could make good sense to pro-ceed along two or even three courses concurrently, given careful attention to the pacing of activities.

☐ The most ambitious approach is to implement a com-prehensive, government-wide formal strategic planning system, with all state departments participating in the development of the strategic plan. The major steps de-scribed in chapter 1 would be followed in developing the plan: confirmation of the mission and goals of state government; analysis and forecast of the environment; audit of organizational resources; formulation of stra-tegic objectives and action strategies to carry them out.

☐ An option following the basic steps of strategic planning but reduced in scope would be either to test the strategic planning approach in selected state departments or with selected issues crossing departmental lines. The objective would be to generate a set of strategies applying to only a limited sphere of state governmental operations.

☐ A narrower, but potentially valuable, approach would be to build on the ongoing policy analysis efforts in state government, applying certain of the techniques of strategic planning to policy analysis, without attempting to follow rigorously every step of the strategic planning process. The breadth of policy analysis might very well increase through the use of environmental scanning, for example.

The first option— implementation of a government-wide strategic planning system—has two significant advantages. First, of course, it is by definition more comprehensive, thus ensuring that the complex interrelationships tying issues together are more likely to be noted and factored into planning. Second, a highly visible comprehensive planning effort, especially when it is obviously a key element in the administration's program, is a means of generating enthusiasm and, perhaps, even commitment among state managers. However, the comprehensive approach appears to be beyond the reach of many state governments for a number of reasons, if what is meant is the implementation of the total planning process at one time. The barriers to across-the-board implementation are serious:

☐ So little is known at the present time about the applicability of strategic planning in the public sector that a carefully paced, incremental approach appears most sensible.

☐ The complexities and tremendous time demands associated with large-scale planning system implementation would put considerable pressure on the resources of most state governments, no matter how strong the commitment of top management. It is unlikely that many states in this period of widespread contraction of governmental bureaucracies would be able to assemble the required central research and analysis staff to generate comprehensive environmental forecasts or to analyze the substantial documentation that such processes inevitably generate.

☐ As has been observed, skepticism of long-range planning abounds in the public sector—a legacy of highly visible failures such as PPBS at the Federal level and the propensity to expect every new approach to achieve wondrous results at the cost of little pain. The orientation and training effort that would be required to overcome such skepticism and to create a receptive climate for the application of strategic planning would be beyond the reach of most states if a comprehensive process were implemented full scale.

☐ Finally, it is highly doubtful that the government-wide planning approach would withstand the political pressure that would surely be directed to a large-scale effort. By its very nature, strategic planning does not, as a primary purpose, generate substantial short-term benefits, although there is frequently useful "fallout." A highly visible, comprehensive effort would be the object of intensive public scrutiny and would be barraged with demands to justify its costs by demonstrable, instant improvements in governmental services.

The second option—selective application of strategic planning—is attractive in several respects. First, of course, it would require fewer resources, in managerial time, central analytical and coordinative staff support, and political capital. It would allow the Governor to focus on those few program areas or departments identified as highest priority to the administration, and it would also enable the executive department to pilot-test the strategic planning design, which could then be further tailored to the unique circumstances operating in the state and extended subsequently to other areas. In the latter sense, this option can be thought of as a variant of the comprehensive approach, different only in that implementation would be paced. Missteps during implementation would be much less dramatic and visible with the incremental approach, hence causing less threat to the total planning program.

As for the third option, issue analysis of various kinds is presently being used to formulate state policies and make the budget planning process more rational. There is no reason to believe that the application of certain of the techniques of strategic planning would not make issue analysis a more powerful management tool. Again, the state's complete planning program might very well encompass the concurrent use of the second and third approaches in order to achieve short-term enhancements in the policy formulation, resource allocation, and budget preparation processes, while also applying strategic planning in selected issue areas. There is certainly nothing inherently contradictory in such a mixed approach, so long as it is well thought out and consciously pursued in response to the identified planning needs of the state.

Adoption of a State Strategic Planning Program

The results of the state planning audit having been compiled and analyzed and the broad options considered, the formulation of a state strategic planning program for recommendation to the Governor would now be in order. At this point, there should be a relatively clear picture of a wide variety of factors that must be weighed and reflected in the state's "plan to plan." These include the Governor's programmatic priorities and attitudes about, and expectations of, planning; the demonstrable planning needs and requirements of the state; the status of current planning in the state and the strength of the management infrastructure that will support planning; the management climate in the departments and the political climate within which planning will be done.

There are no simple rules to follow in weighing the foregoing factors and applying them in the development of a planning design; their relative importance will vary from state to state. The point is to ensure that all pertinent factors have been explicitly examined as a means to assure that the recommended planning design is feasible. It is obviously possible to err on the side of conservatism by exaggerating the barriers to strategic planning, and hence to reap fewer of the benefits that might accrue from the use of strategic planning in state government. This is certainly a risk of focusing on the factors examined as part of the planning audit. Given the history of long-range planning in the public sector, however, the errors of overoptimism and unrealistic expectations would seem to be more serious in their potential consequences. Better, then, to succeed modestly, than to fail spectacularly.

It is recommended that the planning program incorporate certain short-term, visible outcomes in the course of formulating longer-term strategies. This is an important means of building the credibility of, and support for, the strategic planning effort. On the way to more fundamental approaches to the issues being addressed, it is almost always possible to identify incremental operational improvements—if only more effective coordination of existing programs—that will draw favorable attention to the process.

The strategic planning program might be conveyed to the Governor in the form of a detailed memorandum, which would be the subject of detailed review in a meeting including those who participated in the original gubernatorial commitment session that authorized the planning audit and the formulation of the "plan to plan." This planning memorandum is the primary vehicle for securing the firm commitment of the Governor to a specific course of action in applying strategic planning. It is not, however, the more detailed implementation plan that will be required once the Governor has agreed to the major design features set forth in the planning memorandum.

The planning design memorandum will consist of the following major elements:

☐ An introduction explaining that the memorandum is intended to set forth the principal design features of a state strategic planning program, to be submitted for the Governor's action. It should also describe the background leading up to this decision point, including the major elements of the planning audit and the preliminary interview(s) with the Governor.

☐ A section presenting the principal findings of the planning audit and the implications for state application of strategic planning (those features of the planning environment particularly positive and negative insofar as strategic planning is concerned) (see Appendix C).

☐ A section defining the scope of the initial state strategic planning effort, including:

   a. The principal objectives of the effort, in terms of specific programmatic or issue areas being addressed during this planning effort.
   b. The likely benefits in terms of impact on the administration's articulated mission and goals.
   c. The timetable of major planning milestones.
   d. The overall cost, including person-hours and any direct expenditures required.

☐ A description of the roles and responsibilities of major actors in the process, including the Governor, state planning office, departmental directors, and any review or coordinative mechanisms (such as a steering committee) being used.

☐ A detailed start-up timetable of steps to be taken from the Governor's approval of a program to the beginning of the strategic planning process.

This design memorandum is intended to serve as the basis for a detailed discussion between the Governor and key staff; a specific strategic planning program will have been agreed to at the conclusion. The political and technical complexities involved dictate that every facet of the planning initiative be thoroughly discussed—the intended outcomes, the limitations, the Governor's commitment of time to specific activities, and the total costs, to name the most important. Any major unresolved issue at this stage will jeopardize the ultimate success of the strategic planning program.

Next Steps

Once the Governor has made a firm commitment to the critical elements in the proposed state strategic planning program, the following steps will be necessary to ensure full and timely implementation of the program:

☐ Development of a detailed planning procedures manual should be undertaken; it should be ready for distribution by the time the planning is scheduled to commence. Such a manual should set forth the purposes and major expected benefits of the process, describe in detail each step in the process, and explain how to use any forms required (see Appendix D for an illustrative table of contents of the planning manual).

☐ The Governor's cabinet and managers of participating departments should be apprised of the planning effort by a detailed memorandum from the Governor; this can be basically an updated version of the planning program design memorandum prepared for the Governor's review. This might also be an appropriate means of alerting key state legislators to the upcoming effort.

☐ The Governor, assisted by whoever has been designated to oversee the strategic planning effort, will want to brief the cabinet and key legislators in person. It is also advisable for the Governor to address the managers of affected departments at the commencement of planning orientation periods.

☐ Ample time should be reserved for the orientation and training of departmental staff participating in the planning effort. Beyond the Governor's personal statement of purpose and expectations, there should be detailed orientation on each step of the process.

Advantages of the Incremental Approach

During the discussion of the broad planning options, several potential disadvantages of the comprehensive government-wide strategic planning approach were noted. The point was not that a full-fledged strategic planning system in state government would not realize significant benefits; rather, it was that proceeding to build such a system incrementally might be a much more realistic approach, in terms of the resources required, the technical complexities, and the political ramifications. Very simply, the wider the scope of the planning effort, the greater the opportunities for mistakes to be made and the likelier they will be noticed.

The advantages of a graduated approach are so compelling that this approach should be recommended to any state currently considering the application of strategic planning.

☐ The intense personal involvement of the Governor in this initial planning effort will be a critical element in legitimizing the process, and conversely, any withdrawal of interest on the Governor's part will threaten the credibility of the planning effort. The Governor's interest and intense participation are much likelier to be sustained if the planning process focuses only on those few issue areas of highest priority to the administration. The tie between the planning effort and the ultimate success of the administration program will be clear in such a situation, thus making the process less "academic" to the Governor than it otherwise might be.

☐ It is unrealistic to expect constant, strong gubernatorial support for a politically risky course of action if it is clear that the benefits to be realized need not be sacrificed in pursuing a less risky course. Proceeding to apply strategic planning in a graduated fashion without doubt lessens the risk of political controversy. Fewer managers need to be persuaded of the usefulness of the planning effort, the interests of fewer constituencies are affected, and the profile visible to legislators and the general public is much lower.

☐ Technically speaking, anything more than an incremental approach appears ill-advised. The fact is, there is very little experience of successful, large-scale long-range planning in the public sector generally, much less state government, on which states might draw in

127

designing their own strategic planning programs. Although considerable planning of a wide variety of types is being done in state government, long-range planning beyond the traditional physical planning on the urban model is relatively nascent. Furthermore, there are signs that in many states even simple annual and biennial program planning has been largely abandoned as executive and legislative attention focuses on achieving balanced budgets during the deepening fiscal crisis. There is, then, no "model" to guide states in strategic planning beyond the largely private-sector experience, which itself is only now being examined in detail. The development of a reliable model to guide large-scale strategic planning in state government will occur through careful and selective planning experiments, which will supply states with the information necessary to adapt strategic planning techniques more closely to individual circumstances.

Planning System Interrelationships

It is important that the planning design documentation and operating manual not beg the question of the ties—conceptual and operational—between each of the ongoing planning processes in the state government and the strategic planning effort. Merely to overlay a new process without attempting to explicate the links is a sure equation for confusion and doubts as to the seriousness of the new effort. To the extent possible, the strategic planning process design should avoid duplication of existing long-range planning activities, utilizing such ongoing efforts to serve its own purposes. One of the important reasons for conducting the planning audit is to ensure that existing planning is used to the maximum feasible extent in the strategic planning program.

The question of linkages becomes more acute when considering the annual and biennial planning performed as part of the budget preparation process. Whereas few states are probably engaged in comprehensive government-wide long-range planning, all states prepare detailed budgets and most engage in programmatic planning of some kind as part of the budget preparation process. On the one hand, to tie strategic planning too closely to budget decision making would narrow its focus radically, turning it into a type of front-end issue analysis. On the other, to fail to define the tie will signal to participating managers that resources are unlikely to be committed to the strategies being formulated, or at best that resources will be only haphazardly allocated. As was noted earlier, the budgetary process hardly exhausts the opportunities for realizing the benefits of strategic planning, and it is important to examine every change lever when considering how to implement strategies, including tax and regulatory policy as well as the Governor's shaping of program directions, principally through the appointment power.

A solution might be to require that the strategies formulated by the new process contain cost and revenue projections covering three to five years and detailed budget figures for the first year. This obviously requires that the strategic planning cycle be synchronized with the budget planning cycle so that outputs of the former can be factored into the latter.

Structure and Staffing

The success of the proposed strategic planning effort will depend in large measure on the person who is designated by the Governor to provide leadership to the effort. It is essential that the Governor's designation be unequivocal and exclusive and that the requisite authority be delegated. Although the executive responsibility might be carried out by a troika or some other committee arrangement, such an approach would seem to add needless complexity to an already challenging undertaking. It is absolutely required that this strategic planning officer be a senior, trusted associate of the Governor with easy gubernatorial access. He or she must be able to communicate effectively with the Governor and to maintain a close rapport. It is advisable that the strategic planning officer possess such characteristics as political sensitivity and sophistication, keen intelligence, an understanding of the intricacies of bureaucratic administration, and a strong commitment to the idea of long-range planning. In the end, his or her effectiveness will be a function of the level of gubernatorial support; without it, no skills will be enough; with it, personal shortcomings need not be insurmountable barriers to effectiveness (see Appendix E for a sample position description).

If the state planning director possesses the requisite attributes, he or she is probably the logical choice as the strategic planning officer. The strategic planning officer should be provided with the requisite staff support to perform the essential central analytical and coordinative functions, although it is important that the actual planning be done in the line agencies. The level of staffing will depend on the scope of the strategic planning effort. Assistance will be required in the preparation of the detailed planning procedures manual and a preliminary environmental scan and forecast, and in the review and analysis of the documentation generated by the process. If any coordinative or review bodies are established to assist in implementation, staff support will be required to assure their operational effectiveness.

It is doubtful that a formal "Office of Strategic Planning" would be appropriate at this early point in the application of strategic planning; it would only exacerbate tensions and stimulate rivalry while serving no essential purpose. Instead, it might best be treated as a special project, with staff reassigned from current duties on a temporary basis. It is, however, recommended that the staff be located with and report directly to the strategic planning officer. The alternative of the planning officer's having to rely on the support of staff who are at the same time accountable to regular supervisors, and located elsewhere, would contribute yet another hurdle that is best avoided.

The establishment of a strategic planning steering committee chaired and provided staff support by the planning officer might prove useful in the implementation of the strategic planning effort. A variety of coordinative problems inevitably arise during such endeavors, and their timely resolution is important to continued progress. It is also useful to be able to test assumptions and analytical conclusions with a group of knowledgeable executives. Such a committee would include at a minimum the strategic planning officer, the state planning director (if not the planning officer also), the state budget director, the Governor's executive assistant, and the line agency directors involved in strategic planning. It might also be useful to include legislative representation, depending on the political climate in the state. The charge to the committee, from the Governor directly, might include the responsibility to review the detailed strategic planning project design, the environmental scan and forecast, and other major planning products, and to resolve coordinative problems as they occur (see Appendix F for a sample charge).

The Governor's Pivotal Role

Considerable attention has been accorded in the foregoing to the critical role of the chief executive officer in strategic planning. It is universally agreed that the commitment of the chief executive to planning is perhaps the single most important element in its success. If this commitment wavers, the ultimate effectiveness of the planning is called into question. While the words of the chief executive attract attention, all eyes are fixed on the actual behavior of this officer. Any significant discrepancy between word and deed threatens the credibility of the planning process.

The Governor plays no less controlling a role in the strategic planning process than his or her peers in other public and private organizations. It is the Governor who decides on the scope of the strategic planning effort—the objectives to be achieved and the resources to be applied to the planning effort. If the personal involvement of the Governor in the planning process is visible, the likelihood of success is greatly enhanced. The basic responsibilities of the Governor, in addition to approval of the planning process design and the commitment of resources to implement it, are:

- ☐ To take the lead in creating and maintaining an atmosphere in the government conducive to strategic planning; through written communication and active personal participation in orientation and training activities at the cabinet and department levels.
- ☐ To provide the strategic planning officer with strong, consistent support throughout the planning process, being accessible and actively assisting in the resolution of problems impeding the process.
- ☐ To act in a resolute and timely fashion on the strategic decisions that are posed by the process, most importantly the recommended strategic objectives and detailed strategies accompanying them.
- ☐ To interpret to the legislature and public-at-large the purposes, benefits, and limitations of strategic planning, and to take the lead in securing their positive participation to the extent feasible and appropriate.

Early in the planning process, it will likely become obvious whether the Governor places a high priority on strategic planning, and the enthusiasm and quality of managerial participation of others will reflect the perception of the Governor's commitment. The fate of strategic planning over the long run will be largely sealed when the process generates truly difficult decisions for the Governor, requiring the allocation of new, or reallocation of existing, resources, or forcing confrontation with aroused interest groups. If the Governor makes the tough choices in a clear and timely fashion and proceeds to lead the campaign for implementation, and if there are some significant victories—principally that resources are actually allocated to strategic priorities during the budget process—then the prognosis for future strategic planning efforts will be positive.

Politics being the art of the possible, one expects and accepts that in the process of implementing strategic decisions, the Governor must engage in the normal bargaining and compromising, and that some slices will be missing from the emerging loaf. The point is, something significant resulted from the planning process, in large measure because the Governor was willing to take a visible and commanding position on the front lines, and it is now clear to all concerned that such planning merits the commitment of substantial time and intellectual energy.

Legislative Involvement

The nature and extent of legislative participation in strategic planning are complex and sensitive questions, the answers to which are obviously closely tied to the political situation of a particular state. Because, however, full implementation of strategic plans often requires legislative action of some kind, either through review and enactment of the state's budget or other legislation, the Governor and strategic planning officer are obliged to give early, explicit, and detailed attention to the question of legislative involvement.

A general guideline might be that legislative involvement should begin as early and as intensively as is politically feasible. If the state administration maintains a close and reasonably cordial working relationship with the legislative leadership, it might be appropriate to share the strategic planning design document (the "plan to plan") with selected legislative leaders at approximately the same time it is distributed to the cabinet and participating departmental managers. It is advisable that the Governor, assisted by the strategic planning officer, personally review the purposes, expected benefits, limitations, and key elements of strategic planning with these legislative leaders in a suitable setting.

If a strategic planning steering committee is established to assist the strategic planning officer in overseeing, coordinating, and monitoring the planning process, and if the political circumstances warrant, it might be useful to include one or more legislative representatives. Such a committee would serve as an excellent vehicle for structured and focused legislative participation during planning, which, if politically feasible, is almost certain to lay a firmer foundation for ultimate legislative action on strategic objectives.

Even in lieu of a close and positive working relationship between the administration and legislative leadership, it is unlikely that any useful purpose would be served by informing the legislature of proposed strategic actions at the last minute. As soon as planning recommendations begin to emerge from the process, and well before they are fully drafted and finished, it is incumbent on the Governor to take the initiative in briefing the pertinent legislators, particularly the chairpersons and key members of those committees and subcommittees within whose purview the recommended actions will be considered. The more strained the relationship and the higher the barriers against positive legislative action, the more reason to devote time and thought to this facet of implementation. If regular executive-legislative meetings are held to review priorities and policies, it is probably preferable that the strategic planning briefing be accomplished in this forum. In such a setting, the Governor and his staff are advised to focus on the end results, rather than on the process, of strategic planning.

A Case Example

The programmatic area of employment and training possesses several advantages as a means of illustrating the application of strategic planning in a particular issue area. It is concerned with human services, which state government planning has only recently been addressing. Although it may not be on every state's list of the most important issues, it is almost certainly of major importance to all states, including those experiencing both economic expansion and decline. And the area of employment and training is an attractive example because its complexity and the many actors involved at all levels of government make it a worthy challenge to the planning process. Finally, the relative paucity of unrestricted resources available to the states for this purpose forces the exercise of ingenuity and imaginativeness in the formulation of strategies.

The fact that the current Federal administration is committed to effecting radical changes in the Comprehensive Employment Training Act (CETA) program, the major funding conduit for job training activities, makes the employment and training arena all the more attractive as a test of strategic planning. The elimination of CETA as it is now known will certainly increase the pressures on the states to provide leadership and resources to employment and training activities, and the techniques of strategic planning are uniquely geared toward accommodating environmental turbulence.

Since we are in a transition period, with CETA apparently fading out but its successor at the Federal level not yet defined, the following discussion necessarily refers to the existing state and local subsystems created to manage CETA-funded activities (such as the prime sponsors' planning councils). While this approach may make the discussion seem dated, it is conceptually sound since the point is to grasp the tremendous complexity of the employment and training arena and since many of the basic mechanisms are likely to survive CETA's demise.

In order to apply the techniques of strategic planning, it is first necessary to bring the issue into manageable focus by defining it reasonably clearly. In the case of employment and training, although the boundaries are not very precise, there would probably be common agreement that we are referring to those activities involved in assisting people to become employable and to identify and secure employment for which they are prepared. Without doubt, this definition encompasses the activities of the state employment services funded by the Wagner-Peyser Act, of CETA, of secondary and proprietary vocational/technical education, and of the occupational/technical programs of community colleges. It is not commonly considered to include higher education leading to the baccalaureate degree or higher, even though employed college graduates may avail themselves of many of the job training and placement services available through the employment and training "system." Whether related supportive activities such as income maintenance or social services are encompassed is debatable, but it is certain that they cannot be overlooked in the strategy formulation process.

Once the boundaries have been established, it is necessary to determine whether a set of state employment and training goals exists, which might provide overall guidance in the planning effort. At this point in the process, what is required is a statement of desired general conditions rather than specific targets of accomplishment since the subsequent planning is intended to produce such targets. If no such statement exists, it may be appropriate for the Governor to adopt a tentative statement with the understanding that it may require revision after the environmental analysis and forecast have been completed. Since employment and training may be thought of as the human resource component of the broader area of economic development, then the existence of an updated set of state economic development goals is important; at the least, it is imperative that employment and training goals fit within the broad framework of the state's economic development plans.

In the more general discussion of state strategic planning earlier in this chapter, it was suggested that a steering committee might be useful for review and coordinative purposes. In the case of employment and training, the need for a broad-based committee or task force appears acute from the very onset of the planning process. So many different funding sources, administrative arrangements, governmental units, and constituencies are involved that merely "getting a handle" on what the employment and training system is represents a major undertaking. If little or no in-depth, comprehensive planning has been done up to now by the state relative to the employment and training system, it is advisable that the Governor establish an Employment and Training Strategic Planning Steering Committee consisting of at least the following members:

☐ One or two representatives of key employers and organized labor.
☐ State chief administrative officers whose agencies have major involvement, including the heads of the employ-

ment service, the state vocational education unit, the state community college coordinating agency, the state department responsible for economic development, and the state CETA office.

☐ The state budget director and planning director and, if different, the state strategic planning officer.

☐ One or two representatives of local CETA prime sponsors, vocational school districts, and community colleges.

Since the steering committee is intended to be a working group, in contrast to a ceremonial blue ribbon panel, it is important that it be kept to a manageable size, but without losing the diversity of representation necessary for a balanced perspective. It is also important that the committee consist of members able to speak with authority for their organizations—department directors at the state level and chief executive officers of businesses, union organizations, and educational institutions. The breadth of knowledge and creativity required for a dynamic strategic planning process demands very senior level participation.

Illustration:
Environmental Analysis

The first major task of the steering committee will be to review and supplement the environmental analysis and forecast, a first draft of which should be provided by the strategic planning officer. A comprehensive look at the employment and training arena would address the following factors and issues:

☐ The economic picture, including

    a. National trends relative to inflation, levels of business activity and employment, and likely directions of the Federal government in responding to these trends (e.g., tax and budget cutting).

    b. State developments, including current and projected unemployment by region and county, broad structural changes that appear to be underway (e.g., the steady decline of heavy manufacturing in the Northwest and Midwest), along with major job market changes (e.g., declining demand for unskilled manufacturing labor and increasing demand for white collar service employees).

☐ Demographic trends in the state, including total population figures and closer analyses by age group, sex, income and educational level, and by region, county, and major urban center.

☐ Projected education and training needs in light of economic and demographic forecasts.

☐ The resource side: what the "system" is and what it is doing, including

    a. Federal legislative programs and projected changes (e.g., what are expected changes in CETA and support for vocational and community college education?).

    b. State administered programs, such as the employment services bureau, and state-funded and coordinated services, including vocational and community college districts, in terms of levels of funding, types of services, numbers of service recipients, and any available evaluative data on the effectiveness of program activities.

    c. Locally administered programs, principally CETA-funded, not only in terms of the data mentioned in the foregoing point, but also in terms of the operational structure of the local prime sponsors—the committees and councils that have been established, their major responsibilities and operating procedures.

    d. Other potential resources, such as chambers of commerce.

The foregoing outline of the employment and training environmental analysis and forecast merely skims the surface of this highly complex area. The point is to ensure that it is comprehensive in the sense that it incorporates in detail both the requirements and resources of the environment at all levels—national, state, and local. The difficulty will not lie in compiling the readily available current statistics on employment, unemployment, and demographic composition, but in attempting to formulate forecasts and, even more challenging, in assessing the implications of such forecasts for the state. The projection of education and training requirements depends on as firm a grasp as possible of future labor market changes. Informed speculation, while it inevitably results in misjudgments on the specifics, can ensure that a state is not caught totally unprepared by unanticipated needs. The cost of not attempting to fill in the future canvas can be much greater.

One facet of the environmental analysis that is apt to receive less attention than it deserves is an understanding of the structures and processes involved in "manpower system" planning, resource allocation, and operations, and the actual and potential linkages among the various components of the employment and training arena in the state. For example, one of the most important constituent parts of the system currently is the CETA program, which has channeled billions of dollars into a wide variety of "manpower" activities for over a decade, largely through local prime sponsors, with only a relatively small proportion of its resources being funneled through state government. There has evolved an elaborate governance mechanism at the local level for CETA planning and operations, including planning councils, youth councils, the relatively recent Private Industry Councils under CETA's Private Sector Initiatives Programs, and in some localities broader-based bodies independent of the local prime sponsors, such as the Work Education Council. At the state level, there are CETA officers and statewide CETA planning bodies involved in the promotion, with very limited resources, of greater coordination of employment and training resources at the local level and in the building of a more comprehensive data base for planning.

Of course, the precise structural configuration is always changing; at the time this is being written, there are signs that significant changes will be made in CETA, including the possibility of an enhanced state role in the allocation of resources. This does not obviate the need to understand the dynamics of this highly complex mechanism for managing such a sizable financial resource, however, as a means to identify those points where state intervention might have the greatest positive impact. But beyond gaining an in-depth understanding of the workings of each of the constituent parts of the sprawling, diffuse "manpower" system, a complete environmental analysis must also examine the existing and potential interconnections among the many component subsystems. For example, secondary vocational education programs and the technical/occupational programs of community colleges are obviously at different points along the same broad stream. What operating ties have been created to ensure that the flow of students is, indeed, smooth; that secondary vocational training is at least in part the foundation for more advanced work at the community college level? Such links may exist at both the state level—between the community college coordinating unit and the vocational education unit—and at the local level, through direct working arrangements between the community college and secondary school system. The analysis is further complicated by the fact that both of these major components often receive funding from the local CETA program, which can and often does involve them in a competitive situation, providing training to the same basic clientele. In this case, the rough distinction between youth, traditionally served by the secondary schools, and adults, claimed by community colleges, disappears as both systems vie for the out-of-school trainee. And this competitive situation is frequently exacerbated by the enrollment declines that have spurred institutions to launch aggressive recruitment campaigns.

In the case of the for-profit sector, what has been the impact locally of the Federal policy of promoting a stronger business role in planning and operating employment and training programs, principally through the recently established Private Industry Councils? Is it possible to demonstrate active business involvement in the new councils or to pinpoint any significant programmatic changes as a result? Also, what role does the local chamber of commerce or the National Alliance of Business program play in the employment and training system, and what are its links with CETA, the vocational education programs, the state employment service?

The environmental analysis and forecast that has been described for the employment and training area represents a substantial investment of staff time, given the variety of data to be gathered and analyzed and the elaborate network of actors involved in allocating and spending the available dollars. However, the more sophisticated the state's understanding of the environment and how it is changing, the more it will be able to rely on the major assumptions that will be at the heart of the strategies ultimately generated through this strategic planning effort. While it is conceivable that a perfunctory look at the environment—trotting out the usual unemployment figures, inflation prognosis, and broad labor market trends—will better prepare the state to formulate employment and training strategies, it is possible that a shallow analysis will lead to the serious misallocation of resources, in essence to investment in lower yielding "businesses" while foregoing major opportunities.

However, merely collecting as much information as possible without focus can lead to a bulky document that is fascinating to peruse but impossible to use. It is digestion, not just ingestion, that makes the analysis valuable. The "bottom line" of this effort to understand the environment is a comprehension of the following:

☐ The economy of the state—current and forecasted—in terms of national factors that will have significant impact, structural changes that are occurring, and the concomitant labor market changes underway.
☐ Labor force and educational and training requirements associated with the economic forecast.
☐ The employment and training system currently in place, in terms of structure, process, and programmatic activities, including the specific population being served and any indication of the possible effectiveness of services (e.g., What is known about job placement and retention for the various programs?).

☐ Finally, the identification of critical actual or potential gaps between employment and training needs and requirements and the services presently being provided by the system and likely to be provided by the emerging system.

The last point is what makes the environmental analysis a powerful element in the strategic planning process. It is the identification and exploration in detail of the implications of the current and forecasted conditions that lead to the formulation of strategies that are rational, in the sense that they address the most pressing needs in ways that make the best use of available resources.

Illustration: Resource Inventory

The next major step is the state resource inventory, which involves a searching examination of the existing and projected resources of the state that have a bearing on the state's role in employment and training. Although the inventory will naturally focus initial attention on the existing administrative units and program activities in the area, it is important that the inventory be as comprehensive as possible. The approach is best if broadly inclusive, in order that the conventional wisdom not be allowed to filter out potential resources prematurely. Self-discipline is most appropriately exercised at a later stage of planning, when one reaches the point of evaluating alternative strategies.

The state general revenue picture is obviously an important element in the inventory of resources. Given the economic situation and taxpayer sentiment, what is the prognosis for revenue growth? Is revenue likely to outpace inflation, thus leaving some flexibility for the financing of new programmatic initiatives from state coffers? The environmental scan will have looked at Federal legislative directions, which merit a closer examination at this stage in order to determine where contraction and expansion are likely to occur. Related to this is the question of Federal funding flexibility—whether funds can be expected to flow to the states with fewer, or more, strings attached, and what the specific changes are likely to be. The apparent move toward less restrictive Federal block grants as this is being written should receive serious attention in any state's resource inventory; simultaneous reductions in Federal aid may limit the apparent flexibility of block grants and must also be considered.

In terms of its current programming, what latitude does the state have to change operating policies and practices in response to newly formulated directions? A case in point is the federal-state employment service governed by the Wagner-Peyser Act. This extensive network looms large as a state resource in the employment and training area, but its promise for contributing to the implementation of new strategies is obviously closely linked to the potential for changing the existing legislation to enable the state to play a different role in the "manpower" system. This raises the whole question of the leverage that the state can bring to bear in shaping Federal directions. Even though it is difficult to pin down, the state must attempt to assess its resources here in order to be able to evaluate fully the alternative strategic directions to be considered later. Among the more important factors to be looked at are the influence and policy postures of national lobbying organizations to which the state has access, most notably the National Governors' Association, and the historical track record of the state in securing Federal action, either through work with its congressional delegation or direct relations with the executive branch.

To round out the inventory, the state should consider and attempt to weigh the potential of such resources as the A-95 plan's review and comment function, the Governor's capability to shape tax and regulatory policies and to influence public opinion generally and local officials more specifically, the state's ability to convene statewide forums to deliberate on state issues, and the state's natural advantages in such functions as information collection and dissemination.

Either as a next major step, or as the natural conclusion of the resource inventory, it is necessary at this stage of the strategic planning process to array side by side the targets of opportunity that emerge from the environmental analysis and resource inventory and the constraints pertaining to the targets. A no-holds-barred approach is appropriate here since the object is to bring to light as many significant opportunities for state activity in the field of employment and training as possible, along with every conceivable constraint that might limit state action. It is at this highly creative, brainstorming stage that a diverse, interested, and active steering committee becomes invaluable. If the membership consists, as was recommended, of chief executives representing business, labor, and public organizations, and if the staff support provided by the strategic planning officer is of high quality, an impressive list of opportunities for state involvement should emerge from the deliberations.

The next step is to work through this extensive list of possible state directions, eliminating those that promise little relative return or involve resource commitments deemed totally unrealistic, or technical or operational barriers not likely to be surmounted. Another dimension of this analysis is to compare the targets of opportunity under consideration to the existing state goals in employment and training, both to ensure that each target is consistent and to assess which targets appear to contribute most directly to the goals. It is possible that certain of the more sophisticated analytical tools that are used in the business sector in formulating and evaluating strategies can be profitably applied in this process, so long as their limitations are kept in mind and, because they are essentially a matter of human judgment, are not allowed to become a mechanical, and hence less realistic, process.

The foregoing means of identifying and winnowing a list of strategic objectives could, depending on the complexity of a state's environment, continue for an inordinate period unless carefully structured and guided. It is difficult to specify where to draw the line since the ultimate strategies will benefit from the creativity of unrestrained brainstorming early in the process. The preparation and distribution of complete first-draft documents to steering committee members well in advance of sessions is an important way of disciplining the process. Another is to agree at the start to a firm schedule of meetings, each of which has specific objectives. For example, the following schedule appears realistic if staff preparation is of high quality and meetings to the point:

- ☐ First session: review of first-draft environmental scan/forecast.
- ☐ Second session: review and agreement on second-draft environmental scan/forecast.
- ☐ Third session: review of resource inventory draft.
- ☐ Fourth session: agreement to the revised resource inventory and review of first-draft list of strategic opportunities with associated costs and benefits.
- ☐ Fifth session: rank-ordering of strategic objectives for recommendation to Governor.

Illustration:
Planning = Decision Making

At this point, the Governor should exercise a major decision-making role in the strategic planning process. The "product" of the steering committee's deliberation should be presented to the Governor for detailed review and decision. This product is a document presenting the pared-down list of possible state strategic objectives in the area of employment and training and, although detailed implementing strategies have not yet been formulated, each proposed objective should be accompanied by a statement not only of the expected outcomes over the next five to ten years, but also the associated costs and resources to be tapped in meeting them. The costs should be comprehensively conceived, covering not only the monetary resources needed but also such intangible payments as the use of the Governor's political credit. It is important that the Governor have a good grasp of the benefits, costs, and the technical approach associated with each option. It is perhaps advisable that the steering committee prioritize its suggested targets; but whether it does or not, it is the responsibility of the Governor, with the assistance of the steering committee, at this stage of the process to select those strategic targets for which detailed strategies are to be developed.

The constituent parts of a complete strategy have been reviewed in some detail earlier in this book. In addition to identifying the desired outcomes as precisely as feasible, it is necessary to flesh out the structure and process required to implement the strategic objective and the costs year-by-year, with the budget requirements for the ensuing fiscal period worked out in full detail. The implementation plan should set forth all major steps and actions with assigned deadlines and responsibilities. Let us say, for example, that the Governor has decided to apply state resources to the strategic objective of building a comprehensive local employment and training delivery system, with a single community plan as the basis for coordinating and integrating the activities of all principal actors. The strategy formulated to implement this objective should make clear what steps the Governor is expected to take to ensure implementation—what contacts he should initiate, for example, with local organizations such as CETA prime sponsors, community colleges, and chambers of commerce, the timing and context of such contacts, and the required outcomes. If legislation is required, the strategy should make clear when and how it is to be initiated, and what, if any, role the Governor is to play in securing its passage.

It has been noted earlier that strategies should be expected to change as the circumstances leading to their adoption change. It is important, then, that the implementation process be closely monitored and, as significant environmental change signals the need for revising the plan, that such alternations are made in a timely fashion, presumably through the regular budget process since this is the vehicle for the allocation of resources to the strategies. Therefore, only the implementation plan for the subsequent budget period is developed in precise detail, and the revision process does not entail massive rewriting efforts.

Conclusion

This chapter has offered practical guidance in the utilization of strategic planning techniques in state government. The intent has been to walk a fine line between being specific enough to be helpful and being general enough to reflect the conspicuous differences among states in terms of planning needs and requirements and planning experience. There is a principal message: that states have a wide variety of options available to them in applying strategic planning, and that the success of the approach they select will depend heavily on how carefully it is adapted to their own individual circumstances.

It has been suggested that states should seriously consider taking an incremental approach to strategic planning, even if the ultimate goal is a comprehensive, government-wide system. The incremental approach, which basically consists of applying in-depth strategic planning to only a few very important issues, has the advantage of allowing a state to test strategic planning thoroughly in its unique situation and to develop a planning model that may then be applied more widely. The broader approach, given the slim knowledge base and high visibility, entails much greater risk and may very well jeopardize the whole planning thrust.

Successful implementation depends upon the skillful education and management of state personnel. To gain their support, managers must present effectively the central ideas, skills, and procedures of strategic planning through a well-conceived but simple educational effort.

It begins and ends with the Governor. Strategic planning cannot begin without a strong gubernatorial commitment, and the implementation of strategic objectives requires the Governor to make a variety of important decisions in an unambiguous and timely fashion. No matter how technically well conceived the planning effort, if it loses touch with the Governor, it has lost its reason for being; demise is certain in this event, however slow it may be in coming. Indeed it may be no exaggeration to observe, in bringing this exposition to a close, that strategic planning represents the essence of what the function of chief executiveship is all about. Accordingly, it is a management tool that Governors will want to adopt in order to provide strong, creative leadership in their states. If, as is widely believed, the current planning and management practices have proved inadequate to the ever more complex tasks of governing and if the challenges to effective executive leadership will increase dramatically, then the only rational course may be to apply as widely as circumstances allow the principles of strategic planning. It is hoped that this book will serve as a useful guide in that application.

Appendixes

Initial Strategic Planning
Memorandum to the Governor

TO: The Governor

SUBJ: Proposal to Explore the Feasibility of Strategic Planning in State Government

Over the past two years, your administration has significantly upgraded the quality of management in state government, ensuring that efficient use is made of taxpayer dollars. Perhaps our most important accomplishment has been the adoption of a programmatic budget system, which has enabled state managers to focus on the outcomes of their activities, rather than solely on the objects of expenditure, even though we have quite a way to go before this new approach is fully accepted and utilized.

We have appropriately chosen up to this point to concentrate our efforts on short-term management improvements, but it is becoming increasingly clear that there is a pressing need for the administration to extend the horizons of its planning in order to cope successfully with forces militating against state government effectiveness. The state has without doubt entered a period of nongrowth economically, and the dollars available to finance governmental services will almost certainly decline in relative terms for a number of years to come. You hardly need to be told that the process of cutting back our budgets to fit projected revenues is both painful and politically sensitive, and the absence of a long-range planning framework with clear priorities and directions makes the process less than rational. You are certainly correct in your observation that the foremost danger in this period of budget contraction is that we will succumb to the temptation to cut budgets across the board, in grand meat-ax fashion, and hence fail to invest adequately in those areas that might, indeed, restore economic growth over the long run.

The principal purposes of this memorandum are to introduce to you a type of long-range planning that appears to have tremendous potential for the administration's successful leadership during these economically straitened times and to describe how we can go about determining whether, and how, to apply this approach, known as strategic planning. If you concur, the matter will be explored over the next three months and a strategic planning program design developed for your review and action.

Strategic planning may be thought of as a more advanced stage of development in the field of long-range planning, different from traditional long-range planning basically in its focus on the external environment of an organization and on the interaction of the organization with its environment. The major aim of strategic planning is to ensure that an organization adopts strategies that enable it to make the fullest use of its resources in capitalizing on environmental opportunities and in minimizing environmental constraints.

Strategic planning has basically developed over the past twenty years in the private, for-profit sector in response to what is sometimes referred to as the "Age of Discontinuity"—an era of rapidly escalating environmental change and complexity that is apparently becoming less amenable to prediction. Although fairly impressive bodies of theory and practical experience have been accumulated, public sector applications have been very rare, and there are few guideposts to follow. However, there have been enough large-scale successful applications in the for-profit sector, such as General Electric's, to recommend serious consideration of strategic planning for any large organization.

There are four basic steps in strategic planning:

☐ The environmental scan and analysis, which involve identifying, forecasting, and assessing the implications of external environmental conditions that should be taken into account in shaping the strategic directions of state government.

☐ The internal resource audit, which consists of an assessment of the government's strengths and weaknesses in terms of a variety of factors, such as programmatic operations and management depth.

☐ The formulation of a set of strategic objectives (or targets of opportunity) and of detailed strategies for carrying them out.

☐ The implementation of strategies.

The environmental analysis and forecast will result in the identification of significant opportunities for the state to pursue, and serious constraints barring certain directions. Bringing to bear the internal resource assessment will lead to the formulation of strategic objectives that promise significant payoff and are feasible in terms of state resources. The strategies that are formulated to achieve these objectives consist of the important steps to be taken and the resources required, with detailed attention to the budget requirements for the first year or two.

Strategic planning will require a significant commitment of your time, as well as that of participating managers, if it is to be successfully applied, and it would be a disservice to you to recommend that we launch a major planning effort without first giving sustained attention to the development of a planning program adapted to our unique needs, requirements, and circumstances. It is anticipated that such a design process will require three months and consist of the following elements:

☐ Clarification of your needs and expectations relative to state planning, basically through one or two intensive interview sessions.

☐ Inventory and assessment of current state planning, including the identification of the kinds of planning being done—process and product—and a rough evaluation of their effectiveness.

☐ Development of a strategic planning program for your consideration, consisting of the planning objectives to be achieved, the process to be followed, the roles and responsibilities of the Governor and other major participants in the process, and the estimated costs of implementing the planning program.

By taking the time to go through the foregoing steps, we can assure that the planning program that is recommended to you addresses the highest priority planning needs and is technically, economically, and politically feasible. In light of our relative lack of experience in large-scale long-range planning, it is very likely that the planning program submitted to you will propose an incremental approach to the application of strategic planning in the state, enabling us to test the process thoroughly in a limited number of areas before applying it more widely.

Responsibility for the development of a strategic planning program should be entrusted to a cabinet officer in whom you have complete confidence and who has demonstrated objectivity and openness in the past when new management processes and techniques have been considered. If the state planning director is in the position to devote the time and attention required for this activity, then he or she would be the obvious choice. If not, you may want to consider one of your senior assistants who works well with the planning director. Whoever is given the assignment will require the full-time assistance of a senior planning analyst for the three-month developmental period.

As soon as your schedule allows, we hope to spend an hour or two with you to review this memorandum and to assist you in deciding on the next steps. If you would like to read further in the area of strategic planning prior to this session, please let us know and we will supply additional material at once.

Governor's Planning Requirements Interview Guide

By way of introduction, the interviewer should explain to the Governor that the purpose of this and any subsequent interviews is to understand what he or she wants planning to accomplish for the administration, so that these expectations may be factored into the strategic planning program design. The following points are not intended to be mutually exclusive, nor is the sequence of essence. These points are intended to direct; where they lead, and in what detail, will depend on the specific circumstances of the interview.

☐ How is planning seen as contributing to the mission and goals of the administration? More specifically, how is it seen as directly supporting the Governor in his or her leadership role? If possible, detail the distinct contributions of different types of planning.

☐ If it were possible to design a state planning system from point zero, what basic types of planning would the Governor want for what purposes?

☐ What areas of state government are seen as most in need of planning? How would the Governor approach the planning challenge?

☐ Is there a need for assistance from planning in carrying out the leadership role of the Governor? If so, explain what specific assistance is needed.

☐ From the Governor's perspective, what major shortcomings exist in the state's planning arena, and how might they be remedied?

☐ What existing planning process(es) (or what departmental planning) impress the Governor the most, and why?

☐ How much time, roughly, does the Governor devote to the different types of planning, and if the time allotment could be changed, how would the Governor change it?

☐ Describe the Governor's relationship to the state planning office, in terms of where it is most and least helpful, how the Governor relies on it, its access to the Governor, and what improvements the Governor would like to see made in the relationship.

Illustrative Planning Audit Findings Section of the Strategic Planning Program Design Memorandum to the Governor

Results of the Planning Audit

Between March 15 and May 2, the senior analyst assigned to this project devoted full time to gathering information on the various kinds of planning currently being carried out in the state and on the perceptions of effectiveness in terms of impact and direct assistance to managers in doing their jobs. An in-depth, comprehensive survey might have taken a full year or more to complete, and so the findings set forth below should be considered as tentative in nature. Most attention was given to the biennial planning required as part of the regular budget preparation process and to individual master planning projects undertaken over the past four years. However, information was collected by written questionnaire on as many of the more limited planning processes, such as those associated with Federal grant applications, as could be identified.

Major Findings

☐ A tremendous amount of planning is being done in the state government, much of it (some twenty identified processes) in response to Federal grant requirements. There is strong, almost unanimous, feeling that Federally required planning is not closely related to, or supportive of, mainstream state management activities, that it is in large measure a matter of going through the motions.

☐ The biennial budget process does require that managers prepare budget requests by major programs, within which measurable objectives are developed, in addition to the traditional object-of-expenditure detail by organizational unit within department. It is difficult to document that the programmatic planning has played a significant role in the allocation of resources to departments, but there is a very strong perception that the formulation of program objectives has been useful in terms of management of the departments.

☐ The biennial Governor's priorities statement issued at the onset of budget planning has apparently had little real influence over shaping departmental budget plans; the process is basically one of the central planning staff and Governor reacting to priorities articulated in departmental planning documentation.

☐ The horizon of the biennial planning process is definitely very limited; no attempt is made to formulate five- or ten-year goals based on a scan of the environment.

☐ There is no formal, state-wide planning process beyond the biennial budget preparation process, but there have been notable master planning efforts, which are very like strategic planning, by particular departments. The two occurring in the past four years—by the Board of Regents and the Department of Economic and Community Development—are not only apparently one-time efforts, not being systematically updated, but are also connected in no obvious way to regular biennial planning:

    a. The Board of Regents in 1978 developed a document entitled "Higher Education to the Year 2000," which begins with a statement of broad goals, presents a detailed forecast of demographic and socio-economic factors with a bearing on the state's higher education system, describes the current higher education system, and sets forth priorities for future development. There is no attempt to identify total costs or detail biennial budget requirements.

    b. In 1980, the Department of Economic and Community Development published "State Development Directions to 1990," which takes a much shallower look at the environment than the Regents' plan but does formulate more specific long-term objectives with estimated total resource requirements. Although laudable attempts to provide a more comprehensive framework for biennial planning, neither of the foregoing master planning experiments has had a demonstrable impact on biennial planning and resource allocation. Both were undertaken independently of the regular state planning process, and, perhaps most significant, neither was produced with much, if any, gubernatorial involvement, nor were any major decisions requested of the Governor.

Implications

The prognosis for a selective test of strategic planning is generally positive. The biennial planning process represents a firm planning foundation; state managers do participate actively in the process and seem to evaluate the programmatic planning component very favorably. There is an obvious vacuum beyond the scope of biennial planning, and the lack of an existing government-wide long-range planning process is most likely an advantage in terms of implementing a new planning system.

Table of Contents
for a State Strategic
Planning Procedures Manual

I. Foreword by the Governor
    A. Process described herein is the cornerstone of the
       administration's program to ensure most effective
       use of state resources
    B. Your cooperation is crucial to the success of this
       planning test
    C. Strong gubernatorial interest and support prom-
       ised

II. Overview of the state's strategic planning process
    A. Strategic planning generally
       1. Benefits
       2. Limitations
       3. Basic steps involved
    B. State process
       1. Description of each step (with deadlines)
       2. Roles and responsibilities
          a. Governor
          b. Strategic Planning Officer
          c. Strategic Planning Steering Committee
          d. Departmental managers
       3. Explanation of tie to budget process

III. Detailed instructions
     A. Environmental forecasting at department level

B. Assessing resources

C. Formulating objectives

D. Formulating strategies

IV. Appendixes

A. Centrally prepared environmental analysis and forecast

B. Detailed schedule of planning events

Position Description: Strategic Planning Officer

I.   Reports to: Governor

II. Supervises: Senior Analyst and Executive Secretary

III. General Function:

Makes detailed design of the state's strategic planning process; offers executive oversight and coordination of implementation of the process; directly supports the Governor and Strategic Planning Steering Committee in strategic planning.

IV. Specific Duties and Responsibilities:

☐ Draws on the Governor's stated planning expectations and requirements and on the planning audit; develops the strategic planning program design for review with the Strategic Planning Steering Committee and Governor. Based on these reviews of the program design, sets forth the detailed strategic planning process in the Strategic Planning Procedures Manual.

☐ Prepares and oversees implementation of an orientation on the strategic planning process for departmental managers.

☐ Produces initial drafts of the environmental forecast and resource draft.

☐ Provides staff support to the Steering Committee, including:

    a. Drafting the Committee's charge and workplan.

  b. Ensuring that documentation for Committee review is provided in a complete and timely fashion.

  c. Maintaining sufficient records of Committee deliberations, and distributing summaries of main points to Committee members within a week of each meeting.

☐ Monitors implementation of the planning process, resolving problems as they occur, or as appropriate, referring them to the Steering Committee or Governor for resolution.

☐ Supports the Governor in strategic planning, including:

  a. Ensuring that documents for gubernatorial review are transmitted in complete form and in a timely fashion, and following up on gubernatorial decisions resulting from such reviews.

  b. Supporting the Governor's public role in the planning process—drafting gubernatorial statements and speeches, and staffing key planning meetings with departmental personnel, legislators, the cabinet, and general public.

Charge to the Strategic Planning Steering Committee

TO: The Strategic Planning Steering Committee
FROM: The Governor
SUBJ: Role and Responsibilities of the Committee

At a meeting on June 15, I agreed to a pilot test of the strategic planning process in the area of employment and training, based on the attached document, "Strategic Planning Program Design." The planning design is the outcome of a two-month research and development period, during which state planning needs and requirements were examined and the feasibility of applying strategic planning in state government was thoroughly explored. I am firmly convinced that strategic planning, which is described in some detail in the attachment, has great potential for enhancing our capability to use ever more scarce state resources effectively, with greater return to the taxpayers on their investment. However, an incremental approach, beginning with employment and training, has been formulated in order to assure that a planning process specifically tailored to our unique circumstances is developed before the planning effort is extended to other areas.

I have requested each of you to make a vital contribution to this initial strategic planning effort through your service on the Strategic Planning Steering Committee, which will be basically responsible for critical review of the planning design and key planning products and for assistance to the Strategic Planning Officer in coordination of planning activities. More specifically, I would like the Committee to:

☐ Review and comment on the document "Strategic Planning Program Design" and the more detailed design as set forth in the upcoming Strategic Planning Procedures Manual.

☐ Review and recommend needed changes in such key planning products as the environmental analysis, the state resource audit, strategic objectives, and detailed strategies.

☐ Ensure the full cooperation in the planning process of those administrative units responsible to each of you, and assist the Planning Officer in resolving coordination problems as they occur.

The Strategic Planning Officer is responsible for staff support to the Steering Committee, including the development of a detailed workplan for the Committee's review and of agendas for each meeting, the timely transmittal of completed documentation for Committee review, follow-through on Committee decisions, and the transmittal of summaries of main points of Committee deliberations to all Committee members within a reasonable time after each meeting. He or she will also serve as liaison between my office and the Committee throughout the strategic planning process.

You may be assured that I am personally strongly committed to the application of strategic planning in the government and that I accordingly intend to devote the requisite personal time to ensure that this initial application is successful. I expect to be in close touch with the Steering Committee as planning proceeds—to attend Committee sessions at appropriate points and to accord the Committee's comments and recommendations full and prompt personal attention.

Your conscientious participation in the work of the Strategic Planning Steering Committee will be critical to the ultimate effectiveness of our planning. I want you to know that I am fully aware of, and greatly appreciate your assuming, this weighty burden on top of already taxing schedules. Your dedication and loyalty to the goals of our administration will surely inspire all those participating in

this planning effort to give freely of their time and energy.
    I look forward to seeing you at the kick-off session of
the Committee on July 10. Thank you.

Selected Bibliography

I. Books

Ackoff, Russell L. *A Concept of Corporate Planning.* New York: John Wiley and Sons, Inc., 1970.

Allio, Robert J., and Pennington, Malcolm W., eds. *Corporate Planning: Techniques and Applications.* New York: AMACOM, 1979.

Andrews, Kenneth. *The Concept of Corporate Strategy.* Homewood: Dow Jones-Irwin, Inc., 1971.

Ansoff, H. Igor, ed. *Business Strategy.* New York: Penguin Books, 1969.

_____. *Strategic Management.* New York: John Wiley and Sons, Inc., 1979.

Bennis, Warren C. *Changing Organizations: Essays on the Development and Evolution of Human Organization.* New York: McGraw-Hill Book Company, 1966.

Beyle, Thad L., and Williams, J. Oliver, eds. *The American Governor in Behavioral Perspective.* New York: Harper and Row, 1972.

Buchele, Robert B. *The Management of Business and Public Organizations.* New York: McGraw-Hill, Inc., 1977.

Cannon, J. Thomas. *Business Strategy and Policy.* New York: Harcourt, Brace and World, Inc., 1968.

Carnegie Foundation for the Advancement of Teaching. *More Than Survival: Prospects for Higher Education in a Period of Uncertainty.* San Francisco: Jossey-Bass Publishers, 1975.

Chandler, Alfred D., Jr. *Strategy and Structure: Chapters in the History of the Industrial Enterprise.* Cambridge: The M.I.T. Press, 1962.

Cogan and Associates. *Statewide Policy Instruments.* Washington, D.C.: Council of State Planning Agencies, 1977.

The Conference Board. *Planning and the Chief Executive.* New York: The Conference Board, Inc., 1972.

_____. *Planning Under Uncertainty: Multiple Scenarios and Contingency Planning.* New York: The Conference Board, Inc., 1978.

Drucker, Peter F. *The Age of Discontinuity: Guidelines to Our Changing Society.* New York: Harper and Row, 1968.

_____. *Management: Tasks, Responsibilities, Practices.* New York: Harper and Row, 1973.

Galbraith, Jay R., and Nathanson, Daniel A. *Strategy Implementation: The Role of Structure and Process.* St. Paul: West Publishing Co., 1979.

Gup, Benton E. *Guide to Strategic Planning.* New York: McGraw-Hill, Inc., 1980.

Hartley, David K. *State Strategies for National Economic Policy.* Washington, D.C.: Council of State Planning Agencies, 1977.

Hovey, Harold A. *State Urban Development Strategies.* Washington, D.C.: Council of State Planning Agencies, 1977.

Hussey, D. E. *Introducing Corporate Planning.* Oxford: Pergamon Press, 1971.

Jacob, Herbert, and Vines, Kenneth N., eds. *Politics in the American States: A Comparative Analysis.* Boston: Little, Brown and Company, 1971.

King, William R., and Cleland, David I. *Strategic Planning and Policy.* New York: Van Nostrand Reinhold Company, 1978.

Lindblom, Charles E. *The Intelligence of Democracy: Decision Making Through Mutual Adjustment.* New York: The Free Press, 1965.

Lorange, Peter. *Corporate Planning: An Executive Viewpoint.* Englewood Cliffs, NJ: Prentice-Hall, Inc., 1980.

Moskow, Michael H. *Strategic Planning in Business and Government.* New York: Committee for Economic Development, 1978.

Muchmore, Lynn. *Evaluation of State Planning.* Washington, D.C.: Council of State Planning Agencies, 1977.

Naylor, Thomas H. *Corporate Planning Models.* Manila, Philippines: Addison-Wesley Publishing Company, Inc., 1979.

Nystrom, Harry. *Creativity and Innovation.* Toronto: John Wiley and Sons, 1979.

Radford, K. J. *Strategic Planning: An Analytical Approach.* Reston, VA: Reston Publishing Company, Inc., 1980.

The Research Group. *The Legal Basis for State Policy Planning.* Washington, D.C.: Council of State Planning Agencies, 1977.

Schendel, Dan E., and Hofer, Charles W., eds. *Strategic Management: A New View of Business Policy and Planning.* Boston: Little, Brown and Company, 1979.

Schick, Allen. *Budget Innovation in the States.* Washington, D.C.: The Brookings Institution, 1971.

Steiner, George A. *Top Management Planning.* London: The Macmillan Company, 1969.

Steiner, George A., and Miner, John B. *Management Policy and Strategy: Text, Readings, and Cases.* New York: Macmillan Publishing Co., 1977.

Summer, Charles E. *Strategic Behavior in Business and Government.* Boston: Little, Brown and Company, 1980.

Uyterhoeven, Hugo E. R.; Ackerman, Robert W.; and Rosenblum, John W. *Strategy and Organization: Text and Cases in General Management.* Homewood: Richard D. Irwin, Inc., 1973.

Vickers, Sir Geoffrey. *The Art of Judgment: A Study of Policy Making.* New York: Basic Books, Inc., 1965.

Wise, Harold F. *History of State Planning—An Interpretive Commentary.* Washington, D.C.: Council of State Planning Agencies, 1977.

II. Articles, Speeches, Papers, Other Sources

American Telephone and Telegraph Company. "The Bell System Emerging Issues Program." A 1980 company brochure.

Ansoff, H. Igor. "Managing Strategic Surprise by Response to

Weak Signals." *California Management Review* 18 (Winter 1975): 21–33.

_____. "The State of Practice in Planning Systems." *Sloan Management Review* 18 (Winter 1977): 1–24.

Banks, Robert L., and Wheelwright, Steven C. "Operations vs. Strategy: Trading Tomorrow for Today." *Harvard Business Review* 57 (May–June 1979): 112–120.

Behn, Robert D., "Leadership for Cut-Back Management: The Use of Corporate Strategy." *Public Administration Review* (November–December 1980): 613–620.

Blumenthal, Michael. "Candid Reflections of a Businessman in Washington." *Fortune* 99 (January 29, 1979): 36–49.

Bower, Joseph L. "Effective Public Management." *Harvard Business Review* 55 (March–April 1977): 131–140.

Cohen, Kalman J., and Cyert, Richard M. "Strategy: Formulation, Implementation, and Monitoring." *The Journal of Business* (University of Chicago) 46 (July 1973): 349–367.

Dresh, Stephen P. "A Critique of Planning Models for Postsecondary Education." *The Journal of Higher Education* 46 (May–June 1975): 245–283.

Emshoff, James R., and Finnel, Arthur. "Defining Corporate Strategy: A Case Study Using Strategic Assumptions Analysis." *Sloan Management Review* 20 (Spring 1979): 41–52.

Fox, Harold W. "The Frontiers of Strategic Planning: Intuition or Formal Models?" *Management Review* 70 (April 1981): 8–14.

Fuller, Bruce. "A Framework for Academic Planning." *The Journal of Higher Education* 47 (January–February 1976): 65–77.

Gringer, Peter H. "The Anatomy of Business Strategic Planning Reconsidered." *The Journal of Management Studies* 8 (1971): 199–212.

Grundstein, Nathan D. "The Quality of Urban Management." In *The Quality of Urban Life*, edited by Henry J. Schmandt and Warner Bloomberg, Jr., pp. 395–419. Beverly Hills: Sage Publications, Inc., 1969.

Hobbs, John H., and Heany, Donald F. "Coupling Strategy to Operating Plans." *Harvard Business Review* 55 (May–June 1977): 119–126.

Hoch, Standley. "Strategic Management in GE." An address delivered at the Annual Meeting of the Council of State Planning Agencies held in New Orleans, LA on September 26, 1980.

Hunsicker, J. Quincy. "The Malaise of Strategic Planning." *Management Review* 64 (March 1980): 76–80.

Marks, Maurice. "Organizational Adjustment to Uncertainty." *The Journal of Management Studies* 14 (1977): 1–7.

Miller, Danny, and Friesen, Peter H. "Strategy-Making in Context: Ten Empirical Studies." *The Journal of Management Studies* 14 (October 1977): 253–280.

Mintzberg, Henry. "Patterns in Strategy Formation." *Management Science* 24 (May 1978): 934–948.

——————. "Strategy-Making in Three Modes." *California Management Review* 16 (Winter 1973): 44–53.

Mitroff, Ian I.; Barabba, Vincent P.; and Kilmann, Ralph. "The Application of Behavioral and Philosophical Technologies to Strategic Planning: A Case Study of a Large Federal Agency." *Management Science* 24 (September 1977): 44–58.

Murray, Michael A. "Comparing Public and Private Management: An Exploratory Essay." *Public Administration Review* 35 (July–August 1975): 364–371.

Mushkin, Selma J. "Policy Analysis in State and Community." *Public Administration Review* 37 (May–June 1977): 245–253.

Paine, Frank T., and Anderson, Carl R. "Contingencies Affecting Strategy Formulation and Effectiveness." *The Journal of Management Studies* 14 (May 1977): 147–158.

Paul, R. N.; Donovan, N. B.; and Taylor, J. W. "The Reality Gap in Strategic Planning." *Harvard Business Review* 56 (May–June 1978): 124–130.

Quinn, James Brian. "Strategic Change: 'Logical Incrementalism.' " *Sloan Management Review* 20 (Fall 1978): 7–19.

——————. "Strategic Goals: Process and Politics." *Sloan Management Review* 19 (Fall 1977): 21–37.

Rogers, David. "Managing in the Public and Private Sectors: Similarities and Differences." *Management Review* 70 (May 1981): 48–54.

Schick, Allen. "A Death in the Bureaucracy: The Demise of Federal PPB." *Public Administration Review* 33 (March–April 1973): 146–156.

_____. "Beyond Analysis." *Public Administration Review* 37 (May–June 1977): 258–263.

Shank, J. K.; Niblock, E. G.; and Sandalls, W. T., Jr. "Balance 'Creativity' and 'Practicality' in Formal Planning." *Harvard Business Review* 51 (January–February 1973): 87–95.

Shuck, Emerson C. "The New Planning and an Old Pragmatism." *The Journal of Higher Education* 48 (September–October 1977): 594–602.

Stata, Ray, and Maidique, Modesto A. "Bonus System for Balanced Strategy." *Harvard Business Review* 58 (November–December 1980): 156–163.

Vaizey, John. "Higher Education Planning." In *Higher Education and the Current Crisis*, edited by Barbara B. Burn, pp. 191–198. New York: International Council for Educational Development, 1975.

Vancil, Richard F. "Strategy Formulation in Complex Organizations." *Sloan Management Review* 17 (Winter 1976): 1–18.

Vancil, Richard F. and Lorange, Peter. "How to Design a Strategic Planning System." *Harvard Business Review* 54 (September–October 1976): 75–81.

_____. "Strategic Planning in Diversified Companies." *Harvard Business Review* 53 (January–February 1975): 81–90.

Warren, Charles P. "The States and Urban Strategies: A Comparative Analysis." Washington, D.C.: National Academy of Public Administration, 1980.

Weidenbaum, Murray, and Rockwood, Linda. "Corporate Planning Versus Government Planning." *The Public Interest* (Winter 1977): 59–72.

Wilson, Leonard U., and Watkins, L. V. "State Planning: Problems and Promises." *State Government* 48 (Autumn 1975): 240–243.

Wind, Yoram, and Mahajan, Vijay. "Designing Product and Business Portfolios." *Harvard Business Review* 59 (January–February 1981): 155–165.

Index

STUDIES IN DEVELOPMENT POLICY

1. *State Taxation and Economic Development* by Roger J. Vaughan
2. *Economic Development: Challenge of the 1980s* by Neal Peirce, Jerry Hagstrom, and Carol Steinbach
3. *Innovations in Development Finance* by Lawrence Litvak and Belden Daniels
4. *The Working Poor: Towards a State Agenda* by David M. Gordon
5. *Inflation and Unemployment* by Roger J. Vaughan
6. *Democratizing the Development Process* by Neal Peirce, Jerry Hagstrom, and Carol Steinbach
7. *Venture Capital and Urban Development* by Michael Kieschnick
8. *Development Politics: Private Development and the Public Interest* by Robert Hollister and Tunney Lee
9. *The Capital Budget* by Robert DeVoy and Harold Wise
10. *Banking and Small Business* by Derek Hansen
11. *Taxes and Growth: Business Incentives and Economic Development* by Michael Kieschnick
12. *Pension Funds and Economic Renewal* by Lawrence Litvak
13. *The Road to 1984: Beyond Supply Side Economics* by Roger J. Vaughan

POLICY PAPERS

1. *Economic Renewal: A Guide for the Perplexed*
2. *The Employment and Training System: What's Wrong With It and How To Fix It*
3. *State Regulation and Economic Development*
4. *Industrial Policy*
5. *Financing Entrepreneurship*
6. *State and Local Investment Strategies*
7. *Monetary Policy*
8. *Social Security: Why It's In Trouble and What Can Be Done About It*
9. *Pension Funds and the Housing Problem*

STUDIES IN RENEWABLE RESOURCE POLICY

1. *State Conservation and Solar Energy Tax Programs* by Leonard Rodberg and Meg Schachter
2. *Environmental Quality and Economic Growth* by Robert Hamrin

America in Ruins: Beyond the Public Works Pork Barrel by Pat Choate and Susan Walter